MASTERING AZURE AD B2C

A DEVELOPER'S GUIDE TO IMPLEMENTATION, INTEGRATION, AND CUSTOMIZATION

FIRST EDITION

Preface

In the rapidly evolving digital landscape, the need for robust, scalable, and secure identity management solutions has never been greater. Organizations of all sizes—from startups to global enterprises—are increasingly relying on cloud-native identity platforms to provide seamless user experiences while ensuring compliance and security. Microsoft Azure Active Directory B2C (Business-to-Consumer) stands out as a powerful, flexible identity solution tailored for modern applications.

This book is the **first edition** of a comprehensive guide to mastering Azure AD B2C. It has been carefully structured to lead you from foundational knowledge to advanced implementation strategies, equipping you with the practical tools and insights required to deploy and manage B2C identity services effectively.

Starting with an in-depth introduction to Azure AD B2C, the book explores the fundamentals, highlighting key features, benefits, and comparisons with other identity solutions. As you progress, you will learn how to set up and configure your B2C tenant, integrate a variety of identity providers, and manage user flows using both built-in and custom policies.

The book also delves into branding and user experience customization, ensuring you can create user journeys that reflect your organization's identity. You'll find detailed guidance on securing API integrations, acquiring tokens, and building applications that harness the power of Azure AD B2C.

Advanced chapters tackle topics like RESTful API connectors, external claims sources, and token lifetimes. For developers and administrators alike, the chapters on debugging, logging, and security testing provide practical tools for maintaining a high-performance, reliable identity infrastructure.

Real-world use cases in e-commerce, SaaS, and compliance offer actionable insights, and appendices provide a wealth of reference materials, from code snippets to glossaries, helping reinforce your understanding and application of the concepts covered.

Whether you're a developer, architect, IT professional, or decision-maker, this book will serve as a vital resource on your journey with Azure AD B2C. Each chapter has been curated to ensure clarity, depth, and practical application, helping you not only understand the platform but use it effectively in real-world scenarios.

Table of Contents

Chapter 1: Introduction to Azure AD B2C

What is Azure AD B2C?

Azure Active Directory B2C (Azure AD B2C) is a cloud-based identity and access management (IAM) service that enables organizations to customize and control how users sign up, sign in, and manage their profiles across applications. Built on the robust foundation of Microsoft's Azure Active Directory (Azure AD), B2C is designed specifically for consumer-facing applications—delivering powerful capabilities tailored for customer identity and access management (CIAM).

Unlike traditional identity platforms that focus on internal users (employees, contractors), Azure AD B2C is designed to support millions of external users. Whether you're developing a web application, a mobile app, or a service that needs user authentication, Azure AD B2C provides scalable, reliable, and secure identity services out-of-the-box.

Azure AD B2C supports a wide range of identity providers, including local accounts (email/username and password), social logins (Google, Facebook, Microsoft accounts), and enterprise accounts via OpenID Connect and SAML. With full customization of the sign-in experience, developers can integrate branding and logic that aligns with their business needs, providing a seamless and branded user experience.

Key Capabilities of Azure AD B2C

Azure AD B2C provides several distinguishing capabilities that make it suitable for modern applications:

- **Scalability**: Supports millions of users across geographic regions with enterprise-grade performance and availability.

- **Customizable UX**: Offers complete control over the look and feel of user journeys through HTML, CSS, and JavaScript customization.

- **Security and Compliance**: Built-in support for Multi-Factor Authentication (MFA), threat detection, and compliance with global standards such as GDPR and CCPA.

- **Protocol Support**: Supports industry standards like OAuth 2.0, OpenID Connect, and SAML 2.0, ensuring interoperability with a wide variety of applications.

- **Developer Friendly**: Easily integrates with popular frontend and backend platforms using SDKs and REST APIs.

Core Concepts in Azure AD B2C

To effectively use Azure AD B2C, it's important to understand its core components:

- **Tenants**: A B2C tenant is a dedicated instance of Azure AD B2C service that represents your organization. You manage identity configurations and resources within this   tenant.

- **User Flows and Custom Policies**: These define the steps and logic of user journeys such   as   sign-up,   sign-in,   profile   editing,   and   password   reset.

- **Identity Providers**: These allow users to authenticate using various external credentials, including social accounts, enterprise accounts, or custom OpenID Connect   providers.

- **Applications**: Applications are registered in the tenant to use Azure AD B2C for user authentication   and   authorization.

- **Tokens**: Azure AD B2C issues tokens (ID, Access, Refresh) that applications use to verify   a   user's   identity   and   grant   access   to   resources.

Azure AD vs Azure AD B2C

While Azure AD and Azure AD B2C share a common foundation, their purposes are different:

Feature	Azure AD	Azure AD B2C
Target Users	Employees (internal users)	Customers/consumers (external users)
App Types	Enterprise/internal apps	Customer-facing apps
Identity Providers	Azure AD, Microsoft accounts	Local, social, custom IdPs
Custom UX	Limited	Full HTML/CSS/JS customization
Licensing Model	Per-user or per-app basis	MAU-based billing

Use Cases for Azure AD B2C

Azure AD B2C is ideal for applications that require external user access and scalable identity services. Some common use cases include:

- **E-commerce platforms**: Secure sign-up and sign-in for shoppers using local or social identities.

- **SaaS platforms**: Manage user identities for multi-tenant applications with customizable   policies.

- **Mobile applications**: Authenticate users using built-in or federated identity providers.

- **Government services**: Provide secure access for citizens, ensuring data protection and   compliance.

- **Educational platforms**: Enable student, parent, and teacher login with personalized user   journeys.

Example: Basic B2C Flow Using OAuth 2.0

Here's a simple overview of how an application would use Azure AD B2C for login via OAuth 2.0:

1. The application redirects the user to Azure AD B2C's authorization endpoint:

```
https://your-tenant.b2clogin.com/your-
tenant.onmicrosoft.com/oauth2/v2.0/authorize?
client_id=<app-client-id>&
response_type=code&
redirect_uri=<your-redirect-uri>&
response_mode=query&
scope=openid%20profile&
state=12345&
p=B2C_1_SignInPolicy
```

2. The user signs in using the configured user flow.

3. Azure AD B2C validates the user and redirects back to the application with an authorization   code.

4. The application exchanges the code for tokens (access and ID tokens) using the token endpoint:

```
POST                         https://your-tenant.b2clogin.com/your-
tenant.onmicrosoft.com/oauth2/v2.0/token
Content-Type: application/x-www-form-urlencoded
```

```
client_id=<app-client-id>
&scope=openid
&code=<authorization-code>
&redirect_uri=<your-redirect-uri>
&grant_type=authorization_code
&client_secret=<your-client-secret>
```

5. The application uses the ID token to authenticate the user and the access token to call secured   APIs.

B2C and the Developer Experience

One of the reasons developers love Azure AD B2C is the ease of integration. Using SDKs like MSAL (Microsoft Authentication Library), developers can quickly add authentication to web, mobile, and desktop applications. The platform also supports native integration with frameworks such as React, Angular, ASP.NET Core, and Node.js.

For example, to integrate Azure AD B2C with a React SPA using MSAL.js, you might start with:

```
import { PublicClientApplication } from "@azure/msal-browser";

const msalConfig = {
  auth: {
    clientId: "your-client-id",
    authority:                "https://your-tenant.b2clogin.com/your-
tenant.onmicrosoft.com/B2C_1_SignInPolicy",
    redirectUri: "http://localhost:3000"
  }
};

const msalInstance = new PublicClientApplication(msalConfig);
```

From here, you can handle login flows, acquire tokens, and manage sessions easily.

Conclusion

Azure AD B2C offers a rich and extensible identity platform tailored for applications that serve external users. With support for industry standards, extensive customization, and seamless scalability, it enables developers and organizations to build secure and engaging digital experiences.

As we proceed through this book, you'll gain deeper insights into setting up tenants, configuring providers, managing policies, and deploying real-world solutions. Azure AD B2C is not just a tool—it's a foundational component of secure, user-centric application development in the modern cloud era.

Key Features and Benefits

Azure Active Directory B2C (Azure AD B2C) provides a comprehensive and flexible solution for managing customer identities. It is engineered to scale, adapt, and secure digital experiences for millions of users. The features provided by Azure AD B2C go far beyond simple authentication and user management—they extend into branding, customization, compliance, extensibility, and performance. In this section, we will explore in detail the key features that make Azure AD B2C an attractive choice for modern application identity management, as well as the benefits they bring to both developers and organizations.

Scalable Consumer Identity Management

Azure AD B2C is built on the global, high-availability Azure platform. It can support applications that serve tens of millions of users with high throughput and low latency. Whether you're launching a local SaaS startup or operating a global enterprise platform, Azure AD B2C can scale elastically to meet your demands.

- **Auto-scaling tenant services** mean no need to manually provision infrastructure to handle surges in user traffic.

- Support for **multi-tenant SaaS applications** enables isolating data per customer organization or sharing a common tenant with policy differentiation.

- Built-in **throttling protection** ensures service continuity during periods of high usage.

This level of scalability is crucial for real-time consumer platforms such as retail marketplaces, live streaming services, financial dashboards, and public sector portals.

Flexible Authentication Options

Azure AD B2C supports a wide array of identity providers, giving users the flexibility to choose how they want to sign in:

- **Local accounts** using email address and password.

- **Social accounts** such as Google, Facebook, Microsoft, Apple, LinkedIn, and more.

- **Enterprise identities** through OpenID Connect and SAML 2.0.

- **Custom identity providers** including legacy authentication systems, third-party IdPs, or external services.

This flexibility allows developers to support diverse user bases with minimal integration complexity. For instance, a business application might support Microsoft accounts for enterprise users and social logins for freelancers.

Deep Customization of User Journeys

Unlike many CIAM platforms that offer rigid user experiences, Azure AD B2C provides full control over every aspect of the user journey:

- Customize **HTML templates** for sign-up, sign-in, password reset, and profile editing.

- Modify **CSS and JavaScript** to enhance interactivity and enforce branding.

- Define your own **user flow logic** using predefined policies or custom XML-based Identity Experience Framework (IEF) policies.

Here's an example of embedding custom JavaScript into the B2C UI:

```
<script type="text/javascript">
  document.addEventListener("DOMContentLoaded", function () {
    const messageBox = document.getElementById("customMessage");
    if (messageBox) {
      messageBox.innerText = "Welcome back! Please sign in to
continue.";
    }
  });
</script>
```

Such customizations allow branding consistency across your digital assets and create intuitive flows aligned with user expectations and business requirements.

Security and Compliance by Design

Security is a core pillar of Azure AD B2C. Microsoft has built Azure B2C to ensure compliance with global regulations and to protect against modern identity threats.

- **Multi-Factor Authentication (MFA)** can be enforced via built-in policies, with options for SMS, email, or authenticator app verification.

- **Password policies** with complexity, lockout, and expiration settings.

- **Token encryption** and **certificate-based signing** for secure token issuance.

- Built-in **threat detection**, anomaly reporting, and integration with **Azure AD Identity Protection**.

- **Compliance-ready** for GDPR, CCPA, ISO 27001, SOC 2, HIPAA, and other international standards.

Administrators can define token lifetime policies to manage session durations and implement conditional access rules when Azure AD B2C is used alongside Azure AD.

Example of a policy to set token lifetimes:

```
{
  "TokenLifetimePolicy": {
    "AccessTokenLifetime": "00:30:00",
    "IdTokenLifetime": "01:00:00",
    "RefreshTokenLifetime": "14.00:00:00"
  }
}
```

Developer Enablement and Tooling

Azure AD B2C offers excellent support for developers through SDKs, APIs, documentation, and developer tools:

- **Microsoft Authentication Library (MSAL)** for JavaScript, .NET, Java, Python, React Native, and more.

- **REST API support** for programmatic access to user and tenant resources.

- Support for **OAuth 2.0**, **OpenID Connect**, and **SAML 2.0** for standards-based integration.

- **Quickstarts, code samples, and templates** on GitHub and Microsoft Learn.

- Built-in **test environments** for policy validation before production deployment.

A simple login example with MSAL.js in a SPA:

```
const msalInstance = new msal.PublicClientApplication({
  auth: {
    clientId: "your-client-id",
```

```
    authority:                 "https://tenant-name.b2clogin.com/tenant-
name.onmicrosoft.com/B2C_1_signin",
    redirectUri: "http://localhost:3000"
  }
});

function signIn() {
  msalInstance.loginPopup({ scopes: ["openid", "profile"] })
    .then(response => {
      console.log("ID token acquired: ", response.idToken);
    })
    .catch(error => {
      console.error("Login error: ", error);
    });
}
```

This developer-first approach accelerates onboarding and reduces the time required to integrate identity features.

Personalization and Claims Transformation

Azure AD B2C gives you fine-grained control over the information returned in tokens and displayed to users. You can:

- Collect **custom attributes** during sign-up (e.g., phone number, age group, interests).

- Use **claims transformation** to modify, enrich, or validate attributes.

- Call external APIs to fetch additional claims (e.g., user role, payment status).

For example, you could configure a RESTful claims provider to augment the user's token with loyalty status from a CRM system:

```
<ClaimsProvider>
  <DisplayName>CRM Loyalty API</DisplayName>
  <TechnicalProfiles>
    <TechnicalProfile Id="Invoke-LoyaltyAPI">
      <Protocol                                Name="Proprietary"
Handler="Web.TPEngine.Providers.RestfulProvider, ..."/>
      <Metadata>
        <Item Key="ServiceUrl">https://api.mycrm.com/loyalty</Item>
        <Item Key="AuthenticationType">None</Item>
```

```
      </Metadata>
    </TechnicalProfile>
  </TechnicalProfiles>
</ClaimsProvider>
```

This extensibility allows B2C to act not just as an authentication engine but a gateway to user personalization and segmentation.

Global Availability and Localization

Azure AD B2C is globally distributed, offering low-latency access and high availability in all major Azure regions. Key features for internationalization include:

- **Multilingual UI support** with automatic language detection or manual override.

- Custom **resource files** for labels, instructions, error messages, etc.

- Support for **right-to-left** languages and **accessibility standards**.

Organizations can provide user journeys in dozens of languages and ensure inclusivity and compliance with accessibility laws in their operating regions.

Lifecycle and Profile Management

Azure AD B2C supports comprehensive profile management capabilities, including:

- **Self-service profile editing** for users to update personal details.

- **Password reset policies** that allow users to recover access securely.

- **User account management APIs** to enable admin-controlled updates.

- **Audit logging** for user activity tracking and account lifecycle events.

Example of a user profile editing policy configuration:

```
{
  "PolicyId": "B2C_1_ProfileEdit",
  "UserJourney": {
    "OrchestrationSteps": [
      { "Type": "CollectAttributes", "Attributes": ["displayName",
"jobTitle", "city"] },
      { "Type": "WriteAttributes" }
```

```
    ]
  }
}
```

These features contribute to seamless user retention, trust, and engagement over time.

Cost Efficiency and Licensing

Azure AD B2C uses a **monthly active user (MAU)** billing model, making it cost-effective for most applications, especially those with variable usage patterns.

- First 50,000 MAUs per month are **free**.

- Pay-as-you-go model enables startups to scale affordably.

- No upfront licensing costs, making it attractive for proof-of-concept and MVP development.

For example, a seasonal e-commerce site with spikes during holidays pays only for the active users each month, rather than licensing all users upfront.

Summary of Key Benefits

Feature	Benefit
Identity Provider Flexibility	Supports local, social, and custom identities
Custom UX	Full control over branding and flow logic
Developer Tooling	SDKs, samples, and REST API integration
Claims Extensibility	Enrich tokens with external data sources
Global Reach	Localization, multilingual support, accessibility
Security	Built-in MFA, token control, threat protection
Scalability	Handles millions of users, autoscaling

| Cost Efficiency | MAU pricing model, first 50K free |

Azure AD B2C empowers organizations to deliver secure, scalable, and customized identity experiences without compromising on control or cost. As your user base grows, and as your applications evolve, Azure AD B2C stands ready to adapt to your needs, making it one of the most future-proof identity solutions available today.

Use Cases and Real-World Scenarios

Azure Active Directory B2C (Azure AD B2C) is designed to support a wide array of identity management requirements across industries. Its flexibility, scalability, and deep customization make it suitable for a variety of application types and user demographics. This section explores real-world scenarios where Azure AD B2C is applied, breaking down the use cases by industry, business model, and application architecture. Each scenario illustrates how B2C can be integrated, configured, and extended to deliver secure, seamless, and scalable identity experiences.

E-Commerce Platforms

E-commerce platforms are one of the most common consumers of Azure AD B2C due to their need to authenticate high volumes of users securely while maintaining excellent user experience. These platforms often require social login support, custom branding, passwordless sign-in options, and real-time access to user data for personalization.

Key B2C Benefits for E-commerce:

- **Social login integration** increases conversions by reducing friction.

- **Custom branding** maintains trust and aligns with corporate identity.

- **Support for millions of users** ensures scalability during sales events.

- **Secure token handling** for seamless API access to order and profile systems.

Example Scenario:

A global fashion retailer wants users to sign in using their Google or Facebook accounts. The company also offers loyalty rewards, and this information is stored in a separate CRM system. When users sign in, the B2C policy must fetch their loyalty tier and display it in their profile.

This is achieved through:

- A custom policy with a REST API call to the CRM.

- A localized sign-in page with the retailer's branding.

- Multi-language support for global users.

- Secure session management for mobile and web apps.

Claims Enrichment Sample:

```xml
<ClaimsProvider>
  <DisplayName>Loyalty CRM API</DisplayName>
  <TechnicalProfiles>
    <TechnicalProfile Id="Get-LoyaltyTier">
      <Protocol Name="Proprietary" />
      <Metadata>
        <Item
Key="ServiceUrl">https://crm.myretail.com/api/loyalty</Item>
        <Item Key="AuthenticationType">Basic</Item>
        <Item Key="SendClaimsIn">Body</Item>
      </Metadata>
      <InputClaims>
        <InputClaim ClaimTypeReferenceId="email" />
      </InputClaims>
      <OutputClaims>
        <OutputClaim ClaimTypeReferenceId="loyaltyTier" />
      </OutputClaims>
    </TechnicalProfile>
  </TechnicalProfiles>
</ClaimsProvider>
```

SaaS Platforms and Multi-Tenant Applications

Software-as-a-Service (SaaS) platforms often require flexible identity solutions that support multiple tenants (companies or organizations), each with their own user base and configurations. Azure AD B2C supports multi-tenancy by allowing conditional user journeys, segmented branding, and fine-grained access control.

Use Case Highlights:

- Each customer can use their own corporate identity provider (e.g., Azure AD).

- B2C applies branding dynamically based on tenant-specific parameters.

- Claims transformation allows enforcement of tenant-specific roles and features.

- API connectors verify billing status or entitlements on login.

Example Scenario:

A project management SaaS platform serves thousands of organizations. Each customer wants employees to log in using their corporate Microsoft accounts while contractors use personal emails. Based on the user's domain (e.g., `@company.com`), a different user journey is triggered.

Custom Domain-Based Routing:

```xml
<OrchestrationStep Order="1" Type="ClaimsExchange">
  <Preconditions>
    <Precondition Type="ClaimEquals" ExecuteActionsIf="true">
      <Value>email</Value>
      <Value>endsWith:@company.com</Value>
      <Action>SkipThisOrchestrationStep</Action>
    </Precondition>
  </Preconditions>
  <ClaimsExchanges>
    <ClaimsExchange          Id="SelfAsserted-LocalAccountSignin"
TechnicalProfileReferenceId="SelfAsserted-LocalAccountSignin-Email"
/>
  </ClaimsExchanges>
</OrchestrationStep>
```

This allows for powerful, dynamic routing of users to different experiences based on their identity attributes.

Mobile Applications

Modern mobile applications must provide users with fast, seamless, and secure access. Azure AD B2C offers features like silent token refresh, biometric login support (via the platform SDKs), and deep linking, making it ideal for mobile-first platforms.

Mobile Identity Challenges Solved:

- **Device flow support** for smart TVs and consoles.
- **Token caching and silent login** reduce friction.
- **Biometric authentication integration** with local device APIs.

- **Push notifications for MFA** in supported flows.

Example Scenario:

A food delivery mobile app wants to support:

- Social logins for consumers.

- Secure logins for delivery personnel (MFA required).

- Token refresh without forcing users to re-login.

Using the MSAL SDK for React Native or Swift/Android:

```
import { PublicClientApplication } from '@azure/msal-react-native';

const pca = new PublicClientApplication({
  auth: {
    clientId: "app-client-id",
    authority:
"https://yourtenant.b2clogin.com/yourtenant.onmicrosoft.com/B2C_1_Si
gnInPolicy",
    redirectUri: "msauth://yourapp"
  }
});

async function signIn() {
  const result = await pca.acquireTokenInteractive({ scopes:
["openid", "profile"] });
  console.log("Access Token:", result.accessToken);
}
```

Azure AD B2C's secure token issuance process ensures minimal exposure to identity theft or token replay.

Government and Public Sector Portals

Public sector organizations frequently require strong authentication, multilingual interfaces, accessibility compliance, and regulatory audits. Azure AD B2C supports all of these, with options for:

- **Multi-language** user **interfaces.**

- **WCAG** **2.1** **compliant** **templates.**

- **Integration with citizen ID systems** via OpenID Connect or SAML.

- **Auditable logs and reports** via Azure Monitor and Application Insights.

Example Scenario:

A national tax authority offers citizens the ability to log in and manage tax filings. The portal supports multiple regions and official languages, and integrates with a central ID verification system.

With B2C, the portal delivers:

- Multilingual pages with region-specific terms.
- Smart defaults based on user IP address or browser locale.
- Verified login via a government-issued ID (OpenID Connect).
- Full session audit trail and access revocation capabilities.

Sample Localization Snippet:

```
{
  "Localization": {
    "Languages": [
      {
        "Name": "fr",
        "Strings": {
          "emailIntro": "Veuillez entrer votre adresse e-mail",
          "continueButton": "Continuer"
        }
      },
      {
        "Name": "de",
        "Strings": {
          "emailIntro": "Bitte geben Sie Ihre E-Mail-Adresse ein",
          "continueButton": "Weiter"
        }
      }
```

```
    ]
  }
}
```

This data is referenced in the B2C policy files to serve localized content dynamically.

Educational Platforms and Learning Management Systems

Educational apps and platforms, from primary school portals to global online courses, have specific identity needs:

- Support for **student, teacher,** and **parent roles.**

- Integration with **school district authentication providers.**

- **Age-based content filtering** using custom claims.

- Parental consent flows for minors.

Example Scenario:

An online learning platform offers coding courses for children and teenagers. Parents must create and manage child accounts, approve purchases, and track learning progress.

Azure AD B2C facilitates:

- Role-based access management (student, parent, teacher).

- Custom attributes (birthdate, grade level) stored in user profiles.

- Conditional flows based on age, requiring parental sign-up for underage users.

- Custom JavaScript to disable content access for non-verified users.

Custom Attribute Extension:

```
{
  "userAttributes": [
    { "name": "gradeLevel", "dataType": "string", "mutable": true },
    { "name": "parentConsentGiven", "dataType": "boolean", "mutable":
true }
  ]
}
```

Using these attributes, access policies and content recommendations are dynamically generated.

Healthcare and Wellness Platforms

Healthcare apps deal with highly sensitive personal data and must comply with strict regulations like HIPAA. Azure AD B2C ensures this with:

- **Secure** **authentication** **with** **MFA.**
- **Token** **encryption** **and** **secure** **claims.**
- **Audit** **logging** **and** **data** **protection** **policies.**
- **Support for conditional access policies** (when integrated with Azure AD).

Example Scenario:

A telehealth app allows users to book appointments, chat with doctors, and store personal health data. Patients log in using email/password or Apple ID, and all sessions are encrypted and monitored.

Secure Session Configuration:

```
{
  "TokenEncryptionKeyId": "mycertkey",
  "AccessTokenLifetime": "00:15:00",
  "RefreshTokenLifetime": "01.00:00:00",
  "SessionExpiration": "01:00:00"
}
```

This configuration limits token reuse and ensures patient sessions are short-lived and revocable.

Summary of Scenarios and B2C Features

Industry	Use Case	B2C Features Utilized
Retail	Customer login, loyalty tiers	Social login, REST API claims, custom branding

SaaS	Multi-tenant access	Domain-based routing, enterprise IdPs, custom policies
Mobile	Consumer and delivery apps	Token refresh, MSAL SDK, biometric support
Government	Tax and citizen portals	Multilingual UI, OpenID Connect integration, accessibility
Education	Online learning for children	Age-based flows, parent-child account relationships
Healthcare	Patient login for telehealth	Token encryption, MFA, audit logging

These examples demonstrate Azure AD B2C's unmatched flexibility in real-world environments. Its ability to serve different verticals while maintaining performance, security, and customizability makes it one of the most powerful CIAM solutions in the industry today.

Comparison with Azure AD and Other Identity Solutions

Azure Active Directory B2C (Azure AD B2C) is part of the broader Microsoft identity ecosystem, but its purpose, architecture, and feature set distinguish it from Azure Active Directory (Azure AD) and other customer identity and access management (CIAM) platforms. Understanding these differences is critical when choosing the right identity solution for your application. In this section, we will explore a comprehensive comparison between Azure AD B2C and related identity services, both within and outside the Microsoft ecosystem. We will look at architectural differences, feature capabilities, integration models, customization support, pricing, and use cases.

Azure AD B2C vs Azure AD

Azure AD and Azure AD B2C are both built on the Azure cloud identity platform, but they serve fundamentally different purposes:

Feature	Azure AD	Azure AD B2C
Target Audience	Employees and internal users	Customers and external users
Common Use Cases	Office 365, Azure management, internal apps	Public websites, consumer portals, mobile apps

Identity Providers	Azure AD, Microsoft accounts, federation	Local accounts, social IdPs, OpenID/SAML
Customization of User Experience	Limited	Full HTML/CSS/JS customization
User Directory	Microsoft Entra ID (Internal)	Separate B2C tenant
Token Protocols	OAuth2, OpenID Connect, SAML, WS-Fed	OAuth2, OpenID Connect, SAML
Billing Model	Per user/app licensing	Monthly Active Users (MAU)
Multi-Tenant Support	Yes	Yes (via conditional logic/custom policies)
Built-in MFA	Yes	Yes
Custom Policies	No (limited conditional access)	Full user journey orchestration

Architectural Separation

One of the key architectural differences is that Azure AD B2C tenants are separate from standard Azure AD tenants. You can think of B2C as a dedicated sandbox for customer identity, not tied to your organization's internal directory.

For example, your company might have:

- `contoso.com` as an Azure AD tenant for internal employees.
- `contosob2c.onmicrosoft.com` as an Azure AD B2C tenant for public users.

Each tenant is managed independently, and applications registered in one cannot directly access resources in the other unless explicitly configured.

Authentication Use Case Breakdown

Scenario	Azure AD	Azure AD B2C
Employee SSO into Microsoft 365		

Customer sign-up and social login	✗	✓
Integration with internal systems	✓	Conditional, external API-based
Self-service password reset for customers	✗	✓
Branding the login experience	Limited	Full control

Azure AD B2C vs Other CIAM Providers

Beyond Microsoft's own offerings, there are several leading CIAM platforms such as Auth0 (by Okta), Firebase Authentication (by Google), Cognito (by AWS), and Ping Identity. Each solution has unique strengths and trade-offs. Let's compare them based on critical criteria:

Customization and Branding

Feature	Azure AD B2C	Auth0	AWS Cognito	Firebase Auth	Okta Customer IAM
Custom HTML/CSS/JS	✓ Full control	✓ Limited templating	⚠ Partial with hosted UI	✗ (predefined templates)	✓ Custom widget
Multi-language UI	✓ Yes	✓ Yes	✓ Yes	✓ Yes	✓ Yes
Accessibility Ready	✓ WCAG 2.1	⚠ Partial	✗	✗	✓ WCAG compliant

Azure AD B2C leads when it comes to deep UI customization. Developers have complete control over the HTML structure and JavaScript logic, allowing full branding and interactivity customization without being restricted to embedded widgets or pre-configured layouts.

Integration and Protocol Support

Protocols Supported	Azure AD B2C	Auth0	AWS Cognito	Firebase Auth	Okta CIAM
OAuth 2.0	✓	✓	✓	✓	✓

Feature	Azure AD B2C	Auth0	AWS Cognito	Firebase Auth	Okta CIAM
OpenID Connect	✓	✓	✓	✓	✓
SAML	✓	✓	✓	✗	✓
WS-Federation	✗	✗	✗	✗	✓
LDAP	✗	✓ (via gateway)	✓ (via AD connector)	✗	✓
Custom REST API Claims	✓	✓	✗	✗	⚠ (via hooks)

Azure AD B2C is on par with competitors in standards support but stands out with its custom REST API connector support for injecting external claims mid-journey. This is extremely useful in enterprise scenarios such as customer segmentation, license validation, or user risk analysis.

User Management Features

Feature	Azure AD B2C	Auth0	AWS Cognito	Firebase Auth	Okta CIAM
Profile editing UI	✓ Built-in	⚠ SDK/UI needed	⚠ Limited	✗ Custom needed	✓
Attribute extensions	✓ Yes	✓ Yes	✓ Yes	✓ Yes	✓ Yes
Custom roles and groups	⚠ External	✓ Built-in	✓ Built-in	✗	✓
Admin portal for user control	✓ Azure Portal	✓ Dashboard	✓ Console	⚠ Minimal	✓
Self-service password reset	✓ Built-in	✓ Yes	✓ Yes	✓ Yes	✓

Azure AD B2C provides a rich user management model through both the Azure Portal and Graph API. However, its native support for role and group management is limited compared to competitors unless extended via external systems or APIs.

Pricing Models

Provider	Free Tier (Monthly)	Pricing Model
Azure AD B2C	50,000 MAU	Pay-as-you-go (per MAU)
Auth0	7,000 MAU	Tiered with overage fees
AWS Cognito	50,000 MAU	MAU-based and sessions
Firebase Auth	Unlimited anonymous users	Pay for SMS/phone auth
Okta	None	Per user per month

Azure AD B2C is extremely competitive in pricing for scale, particularly due to its generous free tier and per-MAU pricing model. Unlike Auth0 and Okta, which can become costly with overage or enterprise plans, Azure AD B2C allows companies to scale affordably.

Choosing Between Azure AD B2C and Azure AD

When to Choose Azure AD

Use Azure AD when:

- You need to manage employee access to Microsoft 365, Teams, or internal SaaS apps.

- Your identity management involves federation with other enterprise Azure AD tenants.

- You require advanced conditional access, risk-based sign-in, and group policies.

- Integration with Microsoft Defender for Identity or Intune is essential.

When to Choose Azure AD B2C

Use Azure AD B2C when:

- You are building customer-facing applications (B2C/B2B2C/SaaS).

- You want users to sign up using email or social accounts.

- Full control over UI branding is important.

- You need to customize user journeys with REST API calls or complex logic.

- You require scalable and cost-efficient customer identity management.

Hybrid Strategy:

Some enterprises implement both Azure AD and Azure AD B2C:

- Azure AD for internal workforce.

- Azure AD B2C for consumer or partner-facing apps.

This hybrid model ensures the best of both worlds while keeping identity domains isolated for security and governance.

Example: Dual Identity Architecture

```
+-----------------------+          +--------------------------+
| Internal Employee App| <--->| Azure AD (Entra ID)      |
+-----------------------+          +--------------------------+
                                        |
+---------------------------+          |
| Customer-Facing Web App | <----> | Azure AD B2C            |
+---------------------------+          +-------------------------+
```

This separation provides a clear boundary between internal and external identities, aligning with modern identity governance strategies.

Conclusion

Azure AD B2C is purpose-built for consumer and external user identity management. It differs significantly from Azure AD, which is optimized for organizational identities and workforce applications. Compared to other CIAM solutions like Auth0, AWS Cognito, and Firebase Auth, Azure AD B2C offers unmatched customization of user journeys, strong compliance, and cost-effective scaling.

When building digital experiences where user identity is central, Azure AD B2C empowers teams with the tools to design secure, branded, and extensible authentication systems—backed by the scale and reliability of the Microsoft Azure platform. Selecting the right identity platform is a foundational decision, and understanding these distinctions ensures your architecture remains robust and future-ready.

Chapter 2: Setting Up Your Azure AD B2C Tenant

Creating Your First B2C Tenant

Creating your first Azure Active Directory B2C (Azure AD B2C) tenant is a critical first step in enabling identity and access management for consumer-facing applications. Azure AD B2C allows you to build a secure, scalable identity solution without needing to create and maintain your own authentication infrastructure. This section will walk you through every detail needed to create, configure, and prepare your tenant for production use, while highlighting best practices along the way.

Understanding What a B2C Tenant Is

A B2C tenant is a separate instance of Azure Active Directory specifically optimized for managing customer or citizen identities. Unlike traditional Azure AD, which is focused on organizational identities and internal enterprise needs, Azure AD B2C is purpose-built for applications that are accessed by a broad range of external users.

Each tenant is isolated, meaning it has its own directory of users, its own identity policies, and independent settings for applications, identity providers, and custom experiences. When you create a B2C tenant, you're essentially setting up a dedicated space to manage all aspects of identity for your application.

Prerequisites

Before you begin, you'll need:

- An **Azure subscription**: This is required to link your B2C tenant to a billing mechanism and to manage it via the Azure portal.

- **Global Administrator privileges** in the subscription's directory (often your organization's main directory).

- A modern web browser (Microsoft Edge, Chrome, or Firefox preferred).

Step-by-Step: Creating the B2C Tenant

1. **Sign into the Azure Portal**

   Navigate to https://portal.azure.com and sign in using your Azure account credentials.

2. **Search for Azure AD B2C**

   In the top search bar, type "Azure AD B2C" and select the service from the dropdown list. This will bring you to the B2C overview blade.

3. **Start the Tenant Creation Process**

   On the Azure AD B2C overview blade, click **Create a B2C tenant**. This initiates a guided wizard that collects necessary details to set up your tenant.

4. **Fill in Basic Information**

   You'll need to provide the following information:

   o **Organization name**: Choose a name that reflects your project or company.

   o **Initial domain name**: This will be used to construct the default domain, for example: `yourtenant.onmicrosoft.com`.

   o **Country/region**: This determines data residency and compliance features.

Example   input:

yaml

```
Organization name: MyRetailApp
Initial domain name: myretailappb2c
Country: United States
```

5.
6. **Create the Tenant**

   After reviewing your input, click **Create**. The process usually takes less than a minute. Once complete, you'll receive a confirmation and a link to manage your new tenant.

Switching to the B2C Tenant

Creating a B2C tenant adds it to your account, but it exists as a separate directory from your subscription. To manage it, you need to switch to the new tenant:

1. In the top-right corner of the Azure portal, click your profile picture and select **Switch Directory**.

2. From the list, choose the tenant you just created (e.g., `MyRetailApp`).

3. Click **Switch**.

Now you're operating within the context of the B2C tenant.

Linking the B2C Tenant to Your Azure Subscription

Since B2C tenants are created as separate directories, they are not automatically linked to your Azure subscription. To manage resources (like App Insights or storage) from your B2C tenant, you must link it manually.

1. Go back to your **primary directory** (the one associated with your Azure subscription).

2. In the portal search bar, enter "Azure AD B2C" and go to the overview blade.

3. Click **Link an existing B2C tenant**.

4. Provide the **Tenant ID** or select it from the dropdown if visible.

This step allows you to manage the B2C tenant from your main subscription's dashboard.

Assigning Directory Roles to Manage the Tenant

To manage the B2C tenant effectively, assign users the appropriate roles:

1. Switch to the B2C tenant.

2. Go to **Azure Active Directory > Roles and administrators**.

3. Assign **Global Administrator**, **User Administrator**, or **Application Administrator** roles to individuals depending on responsibilities.

Best Practices for Naming and Organization

- Use a clear, concise tenant name that reflects your business or product.

- Stick to a consistent naming convention if managing multiple B2C tenants.

- Add metadata or tags within your Azure environment to distinguish tenants and environments (e.g., Dev, QA, Prod).

Automating Tenant Creation with Azure CLI (Optional)

While the Azure portal is user-friendly, automation may be required for organizations managing multiple tenants or provisioning environments programmatically. Here's a sample using Azure CLI:

```
az ad b2c directory create \
  --display-name "MyRetailApp" \
  --domain-name "myretailappb2c.onmicrosoft.com" \
  --country "US"
```

> **Note:** This command requires special permissions and may not be available in all environments.

Understanding Tenant Lifecycle and Quotas

Azure imposes some limitations and quotas on B2C tenants:

- A maximum of 20 tenants per Azure account.

- Each tenant can contain up to **1 million users** on the free tier.

- Additional users and premium features (e.g., MFA, external identity providers) incur costs.

It is also important to understand that deleting a B2C tenant is a permanent action and cannot be undone.

Frequently Encountered Issues During Setup

1. **Tenant doesn't appear in subscription list**

- Ensure it is linked via "Link an existing B2C tenant."
- Confirm you've switched directories correctly.

2. **Permissions** **issues**

- Verify that the user has Global Administrator or at least B2C-specific roles.

3. **Cannot** **create** **tenant**

- You may hit a quota limit. Check for existing tenants and delete unused ones if needed.

Summary

Creating your Azure AD B2C tenant is the first and foundational step in deploying customer-facing identity management using Microsoft's secure infrastructure. By following the structured process above—setting up your tenant, linking it to your subscription, and assigning roles—you ensure a strong start. Whether you're building a mobile app, a single-page application, or a complex SaaS platform, your tenant becomes the identity backbone of your solution.

As you move forward, you'll build upon this tenant by adding identity providers, designing user flows, integrating APIs, and customizing the user experience. Be sure to maintain documentation and keep track of environment configurations—especially if you plan to scale across regions or teams.

In the next section, we'll explore how directories and subscriptions interact in more depth, setting the stage for governance, billing, and access control across environments.

Understanding Directories and Subscriptions

Azure's identity and resource management model is built around **Azure Active Directory (Azure AD)** and **Azure Subscriptions**. When working with Azure AD B2C, especially at scale, it's essential to grasp how directories and subscriptions interrelate, how they affect access and billing, and how to manage multiple environments securely and efficiently.

This section provides an in-depth exploration of the concepts of directories and subscriptions within Azure and their roles in the context of Azure AD B2C deployments.

What is an Azure Active Directory (AAD) Directory?

An **Azure AD Directory** is essentially a tenant — a dedicated, trusted instance of identity and access management. It serves as a centralized repository for users, groups, roles, applications, and security policies.

In Azure AD B2C:

- Each B2C tenant is a distinct Azure AD directory.

- It is isolated from other directories, including your organization's root Azure directory.

- It stores and governs **consumer identities** instead of corporate or organizational users.

Directories are critical for authentication and identity management, but they do not directly manage resources like virtual machines or databases. That's the role of subscriptions.

What is an Azure Subscription?

An **Azure Subscription** is a container that holds Azure resources (like databases, storage accounts, compute instances) and is tied to a billing account. It defines:

- **Resource boundaries** for services.

- **Billing scope** (what gets charged and to whom).

- **Quota boundaries** (how many resources can be provisioned).

Unlike directories, subscriptions are not identity providers. Instead, they rely on Azure AD for access control. A single directory can be linked to **multiple subscriptions**, and each subscription can be associated with **only one directory**.

Directories vs Subscriptions: Key Differences

Feature	Azure Directory (AAD)	Azure Subscription
Purpose	Identity and access management	Resource management and billing
Scope	Users, groups, roles, policies	VMs, storage, databases, services
Ownership	Linked to an Azure tenant	Linked to a billing account

User Management	Native	Delegated via directory
Isolation	Logical directory boundary	Resource boundary within a directory

How Azure AD B2C Tenants Are Structured

When you create an Azure AD B2C tenant, you're effectively creating a **new directory**. This directory:

- Is separate from your organization's main directory (e.g., `contoso.onmicrosoft.com`).

- Has a different domain name (e.g., `contosob2c.onmicrosoft.com`).

- Doesn't inherit users, groups, or roles from other directories.

- Needs to be **explicitly linked** to a subscription for resource provisioning.

Switching Between Directories

Because each directory is independent, switching between them in the Azure Portal is a common task when managing B2C tenants alongside your organization's other services.

1. Click your account icon in the top-right corner.

2. Select **Switch Directory**.

3. Choose the target directory, e.g., your B2C tenant.

You now view and manage resources within the selected directory context.

CLI Equivalent:

```
az account list --output table
az account set --subscription "<subscription-id-or-name>"
```

You can also change directories with:

```
az login --tenant "<directory-id>"
```

Linking a B2C Directory to a Subscription

To manage resources such as Application Insights or API Gateways for your B2C tenant, the tenant must be associated with a subscription.

Steps:

1. Go to your **home directory** (typically the one linked to your Azure subscription).

2. Search for "Azure AD B2C" in the portal.

3. Choose **Link an existing B2C tenant.**

4. Select or enter the **Directory ID** of your B2C tenant.

5. Confirm the link.

Once linked, you can manage applications, configure monitoring, and provision services on behalf of the B2C tenant using your subscription.

Multi-Directory Management: Pitfalls and Considerations

Managing multiple directories introduces several operational and security challenges:

- **Role Management**: Roles are not portable between directories. You must reassign admin roles in each directory.

- **Portal Confusion**: Switching directories often leads to confusion over missing resources or access errors.

- **Automations and CI/CD**: Scripts must account for changing directory context using explicit tenant IDs.

Best Practice: Use consistent naming conventions and tag resources with environment-specific identifiers.

Role Assignments Across Directories

You can only assign Azure roles (like Reader, Contributor, Owner) to users within the directory that owns the subscription. This means:

- If you want someone to manage resources in the subscription tied to your B2C tenant, they must have an account in that directory.

- Conversely, users in your main organizational directory cannot directly manage the B2C tenant unless added as **guest** **users**.

To add a user from another directory:

1. Go to **Azure** **Active** **Directory** > **Users** > **New** **Guest** **User.**

2. Provide the external user's email and invitation message.

3. Assign appropriate roles once the user accepts.

Subscription and Directory Migration Scenarios

It's not uncommon to start with resources in one directory and later decide to consolidate or migrate them.

Some options:

- **Move subscriptions** between directories using Microsoft support (limited scenarios).

- **Recreate resources** under a new subscription in a different directory.

- **Delegate access** via guest accounts and RBAC (less ideal for large-scale resource movement).

CLI:

```
az account management-group subscription add --name <mg-name> --subscription <subscription-id>
```

Note: Not all services support directory changes. Recreating infrastructure may be necessary.

Directory Governance in Enterprise B2C Deployments

Larger organizations typically adopt governance models for managing directories:

- **Single Directory with Multiple Subscriptions**: Ideal for clear administrative control, centralized billing, and simplified RBAC.

- **Multiple Directories for Each Environment**: Useful for total isolation but requires additional setup and switching effort.

Suggested Structure:

- **Directory 1**: Corporate directory (billing, shared services)

- **Directory 2**: B2C Development

- **Directory 3**: B2C Staging

- **Directory 4**: B2C Production

Each B2C directory can be linked to separate subscriptions for billing and access tracking.

Billing and Resource Isolation

Azure charges are incurred based on subscriptions, not directories. However, directories determine **who** can access those resources.

To optimize billing:

- Use **separate subscriptions** for dev/test environments.

- Use **tags** for cost tracking (e.g., Environment: Production, Project: MyApp).

- Use **management groups** to enforce policy and aggregate billing across subscriptions.

Programmatic Access to Directory Information

You can retrieve directory and subscription info via Azure CLI:

```
az account show --output json
az ad signed-in-user show
az ad tenant list
```

To get the tenant ID of the current session:

```
az account show --query tenantId
```

To find subscriptions under a tenant:

```
az account list --query "[].{Name:name, SubscriptionId:id, TenantId:tenantId}" --output table
```

These are useful in automation scripts and CI/CD pipelines to verify context and permissions.

Summary

Understanding the distinction and interplay between directories and subscriptions is fundamental to managing Azure AD B2C effectively. Directories govern identity, security, and policy enforcement, while subscriptions govern resource allocation and billing. By strategically linking your B2C tenants to the right subscriptions, and adopting a disciplined directory switching and access management model, you can ensure both security and operational efficiency.

Whether you're deploying B2C in a startup with a single app or across an enterprise with hundreds of identity experiences, mastering these foundational concepts is key to maintaining a scalable, secure, and auditable identity solution in Azure.

Assigning Roles and Permissions

Properly assigning roles and permissions is a critical aspect of managing an Azure AD B2C tenant. Without adequate control over who can do what within your tenant and associated Azure resources, you risk unintentional misconfigurations, security breaches, or administrative bottlenecks. Azure provides a robust Role-Based Access Control (RBAC) system that helps manage access to resources securely and with granularity.

This section will explore the different types of roles in Azure, how to assign them, best practices for delegation, the distinction between tenant-level and subscription-level permissions, and how to manage permissions at scale in enterprise environments.

Understanding Role-Based Access Control (RBAC)

Azure's RBAC model allows you to manage **who has access to what resources** and **what they can do with them**. Permissions are assigned to **users**, **groups**, or **service principals** by granting **roles** at specific scopes.

Key Concepts:

- **Role**: A collection of permissions (e.g., Reader, Contributor, Owner).

- **Scope**: The level at which access is granted (e.g., subscription, resource group, resource).

- **Assignment**: A link between a principal (user/service) and a role at a scope.

Example: Assigning the **Contributor** role to a user at the subscription level allows them to manage all resources in that subscription but not grant access to others.

Role Types in Azure AD B2C

There are two main role models to be aware of:

1. **Azure** **Roles** (Subscription Scope)

2. **Azure** **AD** **Roles** (Tenant Scope)

Azure Roles

These are used for managing Azure resources like App Services, APIs, Key Vaults, etc., and apply at the **subscription**, **resource group**, or **individual resource** level.

Examples:

- Owner

- Contributor

- Reader

Azure AD Roles

These roles apply to the Azure AD directory and control identity-related actions such as managing users, assigning licenses, or creating applications.

Examples:

- Global   Administrator

- User   Administrator

- Application   Administrator

- Security   Reader

- Conditional   Access   Administrator

Azure AD B2C uses **Azure AD roles** to manage access within the B2C tenant. Therefore, even though B2C is accessed via the Azure portal, its access model is based on Azure AD roles.

Assigning Directory Roles in Azure AD B2C

After creating your B2C tenant and switching to its directory, you will often need to assign roles to users (e.g., other administrators, developers, auditors). Here's how:

Portal Method:

1. Navigate   to   **Azure   Active   Directory**   in   the   B2C   tenant.

2. Select   **Roles**   **and**   **administrators**.

3. Choose   a   role   (e.g.,   **Global   Administrator**).

4. Click   **Add**   **assignments**.

5. Search   for   and   select   the   user(s).

6. Confirm   the   assignment.

Important Roles for B2C Management:

Role	Purpose
Global Administrator	Full access to manage everything
B2C IEF Policy Administrator	Can create/edit Identity Experience Framework policies
Application Administrator	Can register and manage applications

User Administrator	Manage users and groups
Security Reader	Read-only access to security settings

Using Azure CLI to Assign Roles

You can also assign roles programmatically with Azure CLI:

```
az role assignment create \
  --assignee "<user-object-id>" \
  --role "Contributor" \
  --scope "/subscriptions/<subscription-id>"
```

Or for Azure AD roles (using Microsoft Graph or PowerShell):

```
Connect-AzureAD
Add-AzureADDirectoryRoleMember -ObjectId <RoleObjectId> -RefObjectId <UserObjectId>
```

To list available directory roles:

```
Get-AzureADDirectoryRole
```

Assigning Roles to Guest Users

Often, users in your primary organization directory need access to manage the B2C tenant. Since B2C tenants are isolated directories, these users must be added as **guests**.

Steps:

1. Go to **Users** in the B2C tenant directory.
2. Click **New guest user**.
3. Enter their email address.
4. Send the invitation.

5. Once accepted, assign the appropriate Azure AD role to the guest.

This process allows administrators or developers from another tenant to securely collaborate on B2C configuration.

Managing Roles with Groups

Instead of assigning roles to individual users, it's better to manage permissions via **Azure AD groups**. This approach provides centralized management, auditability, and ease of access changes.

Example:

1. Create a group named `B2C-Policy-Admins`.

2. Assign `B2C IEF Policy Administrator` role to the group.

3. Add/remove users from the group as needed.

This method scales well in enterprise environments with multiple admins.

Delegating Application Management

Applications (SPAs, APIs, mobile apps) registered in B2C often need to be maintained by developers or DevOps teams. Assigning them **Application Administrator** or **Cloud Application Administrator** roles allows this without granting full control over the tenant.

For least privilege:

- Assign Application Administrator for full app management.

- Assign App Registration Reader for read-only access to configurations.

You can also scope access to **specific applications** using custom roles and Graph API, although this is more advanced and typically used in regulated environments.

Access to Custom Policies and Identity Experience Framework (IEF)

To manage custom policies (e.g., TrustFrameworkExtensions.xml), the user must have the `B2C IEF Policy Administrator` role. Without this, access to upload/edit policies will be denied, even if the user is a Global Administrator in a different directory.

Be sure to:

- Enable the **Identity Experience Framework** blade via Azure portal preview features.

- Assign the correct role to users or groups.

- Limit this access to experienced identity engineers or trusted developers due to the sensitive nature of policy logic.

Using Privileged Identity Management (PIM)

If you want to manage role activation with time-bound or approval-based access, enable **Azure AD Privileged Identity Management (PIM)**. This adds governance features like:

- Just-in-time role activation

- Approval workflows

- Audit logs and alerts

- Access reviews

PIM is available on **Azure AD Premium P2** plans and is especially useful in production environments with multiple teams.

Auditing and Logging Role Changes

Access control is only secure if it's auditable. Azure provides several ways to monitor role assignments and changes:

- **Azure AD Audit Logs**: Logs user and admin actions.

- **Azure Activity Logs**: Tracks subscription-level resource activity.

- **Microsoft Graph API**: Programmatically query logs and role assignments.

Example Query with Graph Explorer:

```
GET https://graph.microsoft.com/v1.0/auditLogs/directoryAudits
```

For security, ensure that role changes are reviewed regularly, especially in B2C tenants used in sensitive applications like banking, healthcare, or government platforms.

Best Practices Summary

1. **Use groups for role assignments** – easier to manage and audit.

2. **Follow the principle of least privilege** – assign only necessary roles.

3. **Document role responsibilities** – clarity avoids misconfiguration.

4. **Enable PIM for sensitive roles** – enhances control and reduces risk.

5. **Regularly audit permissions** – look for unnecessary or unused assignments.

6. **Separate development and production roles** – prevent accidental changes.

7. **Use guest access strategically** – reduce the number of full directory users.

Summary

Assigning roles and permissions in Azure AD B2C is a foundational step in establishing secure, efficient, and scalable identity solutions. Whether managing simple apps or enterprise-scale deployments, understanding how to use RBAC at both the Azure subscription and directory level enables fine-grained control and minimizes risk.

By leveraging built-in roles, groups, PIM, and audit logs, organizations can implement governance frameworks that support collaboration while maintaining strong security postures. With these capabilities in place, your B2C tenant becomes not just functional but also trustworthy, manageable, and compliant with modern enterprise standards.

Navigating the Azure Portal for B2C

Effectively managing an Azure AD B2C tenant requires familiarity with the Azure Portal, which serves as the primary graphical user interface for configuring, monitoring, and deploying identity-related services. The Azure Portal is a web-based application that provides a rich experience for interacting with Azure resources, and understanding its structure and B2C-specific areas is critical for both day-to-day operations and strategic architecture.

This section serves as a comprehensive guide to using the Azure Portal for B2C, from logging in and switching directories, to configuring advanced features like user flows, API connectors, and custom policies.

Accessing the Azure Portal

To begin, open your preferred modern browser and navigate to:

```
https://portal.azure.com
```

Sign in using your Azure account credentials. This account must be associated with a directory and have appropriate permissions (e.g., Global Administrator or Application Administrator) to access and manage the B2C tenant.

Once authenticated, the portal loads your home directory by default. If your B2C tenant is in a different directory, you'll need to switch to it to manage it effectively.

Switching to the B2C Tenant Directory

Because B2C tenants are separate directories from your default Azure directory, you'll need to switch to the appropriate tenant context.

1. In the top-right corner, click your **profile avatar**.

2. Select **Switch Directory**.

3. Choose your B2C directory (e.g., `myb2ctenant.onmicrosoft.com`).

4. Wait for the portal to reload in the new directory context.

You now have access to the services and configurations related to the B2C tenant.

CLI Equivalent:

```
az login --tenant <b2c-tenant-id>
```

Or use `az account set` after listing available accounts:

```
az account list --output table
```

```
az account set --subscription <subscription-id>
```

Finding the Azure AD B2C Blade

Once you're in the correct directory:

1. In the left-hand menu, select **All Services**.

2. Search for and select **Azure AD B2C**.

3. Pin it to your dashboard for easier future access.

This will open the Azure AD B2C **Overview blade**, which serves as the entry point for all B2C management features.

Overview Blade Breakdown

The Overview blade gives a summarized view of your B2C tenant. It includes:

- **Tenant** name and domain
- **Directory** (tenant) ID
- **Pricing** tier and region
- **Links** to key features:
  - User flows
  - Identity providers
  - Applications
  - Users
  - Audit logs

From here, you can access the deeper configuration options of your B2C environment.

User Management in Azure Portal

To manage consumer identities:

1. Go to **Azure AD B2C > Users**.

2. You'll see a list of user accounts registered with your tenant.

3. Click on any user to:

   - View profile details

   - Reset passwords

   - Block sign-in

   - Delete the account

You can also create new users manually (for testing) or invite users using **sign-up user flows**.

User Object Properties:

- `UserPrincipalName` (e.g., `user@myb2ctenant.onmicrosoft.com`)

- `ObjectId` (globally unique identifier)

- `SignInNames` (e.g., email, username)

- `Custom Attributes` (if extended via IEF)

Application Registration

To allow apps (e.g., SPAs, APIs) to authenticate via B2C:

1. Go to **Azure AD B2C > App registrations**.

2. Click **New registration**.

3. Configure:

   - Name

   - Redirect URIs (e.g., `https://myapp.com/auth`)

   - Supported account types (only accounts in this tenant)

4. After registering, configure API permissions and expose APIs if needed.

This is foundational for all client applications using B2C for authentication and authorization.

Sample Redirect URI for mobile:

```
com.myappname://oauthredirect
```

User Flows (Built-in Policies)

User flows define pre-configured, customizable identity experiences (e.g., sign-up, sign-in, password reset).

1. Navigate to **Azure AD B2C > User flows**.

2. Click **+ New user flow**.

3. Select the desired flow type:

   - Sign up and sign in

   - Password reset

   - Profile editing

4. Provide a name and select attributes (e.g., email, displayName).

5. Create the flow.

Once created, you can:

- **Run the user flow** (test experience)

- **Edit page layouts and branding**

- **Link the flow to applications**

User flows are ideal for most use cases unless custom logic is required.

Custom Policies (Identity Experience Framework)

For advanced scenarios like custom claims, external REST calls, or UI customization beyond user flows:

1. Enable the **Identity Experience Framework (IEF)** in **Azure AD B2C > Identity Experience   Framework**.

2. Upload   policy   files:

   o `TrustFrameworkBase.xml`

   o `TrustFrameworkExtensions.xml`

   o `SignUpOrSignin.xml`

3. Define   technical   profiles   and   orchestration   steps   within   XML.

Policies are deployed as sets (base + extension + orchestration policy). A consistent naming convention and version control system are highly recommended.

Tips:

- Use **Azure Blob Storage** or GitHub for policy file source control.

- Always   validate   policies   before   applying   in   production.

Identity Providers Configuration

To add third-party identity providers:

1. Go   to   **Azure   AD   B2C   >   Identity   providers**.

2. Choose   from   built-in   providers:

   o Google

   o Facebook

   o Microsoft

3. Provide   client   ID   and   secret   from   the   provider's   developer   console.

4. Save   and   link   the   provider   to   your   user   flows.

Custom providers using **OpenID Connect** or **SAML** can also be configured under the **Identity providers** blade with advanced metadata options.

API Connectors

API Connectors allow you to inject external API calls during user journeys (only in user flows, not IEF yet).

1. Go to **Azure AD B2C > API connectors**.

2. Click + **New API connector**.

3. Define:

    o URL

    o Authentication (basic, certificate, etc.)

    o Timeout and retry settings

After setup, attach the API to specific orchestration steps in a user flow (e.g., validate email domain during sign-up).

Monitoring and Logs

To monitor the health and performance of your B2C tenant:

- Go to **Azure AD B2C > Audit logs**:

    o Tracks actions like user creation, flow execution, policy updates.

- Integrate **Application Insights** for deeper analysis:

    o User journeys

    o Page load times

    o API call success/failure rates

You can stream logs to **Log Analytics**, **Event Hubs**, or **Storage Accounts** for long-term storage or integration with SIEM tools.

Kusto Query Example:

```
AuditLogs
| where OperationName == "UserLoginSuccess"
| summarize Count = count() by bin(TimeGenerated, 1h)
```

Navigating Across Environments (Dev, Test, Prod)

It's common to have multiple B2C tenants for different stages:

- `myapp-dev.onmicrosoft.com`

- `myapp-test.onmicrosoft.com`

- `myapp-prod.onmicrosoft.com`

To manage them efficiently:

- Use browser profiles or incognito sessions to switch between environments.

Maintain bookmarks for each portal tenant URL:

ruby

```
https://portal.azure.com/#@myapp-prod.onmicrosoft.com
```

-
- Leverage automation (ARM templates, Bicep, Terraform) to deploy consistent configurations across environments.

Keyboard Shortcuts and Productivity Tips

- **Ctrl + /:** Open command palette (search across Azure)
- **g + d:** Go to Dashboard
- **g + a:** Go to All Services
- **/ (forward slash):** Focus the search bar

Customizing the dashboard with pinned B2C resources can significantly reduce navigation time.

Common Issues and Fixes

Issue	Resolution
User flow not appearing in app	Ensure app is linked in **User flows > Properties > Applications**
API Connector not calling	Confirm HTTPS endpoint, validate certificate, check response format
Cannot switch directory	Ensure your account has access to the target directory
Cannot upload custom policy	Validate XML schema, use correct policy keys

Summary

Navigating the Azure Portal effectively is vital to mastering Azure AD B2C. From switching tenants and managing users, to configuring user flows and integrating APIs, the portal provides a comprehensive and centralized way to control your identity platform.

As you build, maintain, and scale your B2C solution, becoming fluent in the portal's layout, blades, and features will save time, reduce errors, and empower your team to manage complex identity systems with confidence.

Chapter 3: Configuring Identity Providers

Built-in Local Accounts Setup

Azure AD B2C supports local accounts, which allow users to sign up and sign in using credentials such as email address, username, or phone number with a password. This is an essential feature for applications that need a standalone identity system without relying on external social providers. Setting up local accounts involves configuring identity providers, user flows, and UI customization for a smooth user experience.

Overview of Local Accounts

Local accounts are managed entirely within your Azure AD B2C tenant. They are stored in the directory and can include any combination of email address, username, or phone number as the sign-in identifier. Passwords are hashed and stored securely, and policies can be applied for password strength and account lockout.

Azure AD B2C supports several types of local account identifiers:

- Email   address   (e.g.,   user@example.com)

- Username   (e.g.,   johndoe)

- Phone   number   (e.g.,   +441234567890)

Choosing which identifiers to support depends on your user base and UX requirements. You can allow multiple identifiers within a single policy or restrict to one.

Prerequisites

Before you begin:

- You   must   have   an   Azure   AD   B2C   tenant.

- You   need   a   user   flow   (sign-up   or   sign-in)   or   custom   policy   configured.

- You   need   at   least   Contributor   access   on   the   tenant.

Step-by-Step Setup

1. Register an Application

The first step is to register your application in the B2C tenant. This allows it to interact with Azure AD B2C and defines the redirect URIs for sign-in and sign-up.

1. Go to the **Azure** portal.

2. Navigate to **Azure AD B2C > App registrations**.

3. Click **New registration**.

4. Enter a name (e.g., "MyApp").

5. Set **Supported account types** to "Accounts in this organizational directory only".

6. Enter a redirect URI (e.g., `https://localhost:3000/auth`).

7. Click **Register**.

2. Create a User Flow

To allow users to sign up or sign in with a local account, you must create a user flow.

1. Go to **Azure AD B2C > User flows**.

2. Click **+ New user flow**.

3. Choose the **Sign up and sign in** flow.

4. Give it a name (e.g., `B2C_1_SignUpSignInLocal`).

5. Under **Identity providers**, select **Email signup** or **Username signup**.

6. Choose **Attributes** you want to collect and return (e.g., Display Name, Email, etc.).

7. Click **Create**.

3. Customize Local Account Settings

Once the user flow is created, you can configure how users interact with local accounts:

- Under **Authentication methods**, you can allow or disallow email, username, or phone.

- Under **Page layouts**, customize UI elements such as logo, background color, and button styles.

- Optionally enable reCAPTCHA to protect against bot sign-ups.

4. Configure Password Policies

Azure AD B2C includes built-in password protection policies. These policies help enforce strong security practices:

- Minimum password length

- Required character types (uppercase, numbers, symbols)

- Lockout settings after multiple failed attempts

To configure password policies:

1. Go to the user flow you created.

2. Click **Properties**.

3. Under **User input**, click **Password requirements**.

4. Define your password policy.

Example (custom policy XML snippet):

```
<Password>
  <MinLength>8</MinLength>
  <MaxLength>64</MaxLength>
  <UppercaseRequired>true</UppercaseRequired>
  <LowercaseRequired>true</LowercaseRequired>
  <NumberRequired>true</NumberRequired>
  <SymbolRequired>true</SymbolRequired>
</Password>
```

5. Testing the User Flow

Once configured:

1. Go to the **User flows** section.

2. Select your user flow.

3. Click **Run user flow**.

4. Choose your registered application and redirect URI.

5. A browser window opens showing the local account sign-up/sign-in form.

Try registering with an email and password. If successful, you should be redirected to your app's redirect URI with an access token and ID token.

Handling Email Verification

Azure AD B2C automatically sends a verification email during sign-up. This helps validate the identity of users before account creation.

- You can customize the email template via **Azure AD B2C > User flows > Email**.

- You can configure a **custom sender domain** via **Verified Domains** in the Azure AD blade.

Optional: Enable Phone Sign-Up

In addition to email, you can enable sign-in/sign-up with a phone number:

1. Edit the user flow.

2. Under **Identity providers**, enable **Phone signup**.

3. Azure AD B2C will use SMS-based one-time codes to validate the phone number.

You must configure SMS providers under **Company branding > Multifactor authentication > SMS provider**.

Managing Users with Local Accounts

Azure AD B2C includes a user management interface:

- Navigate to **Azure AD B2C > Users**.

- Filter by sign-in type (local accounts only).

- View user profile, reset password, or delete account.

You can also manage users programmatically using Microsoft Graph API:

```
GET https://graph.microsoft.com/v1.0/users
Authorization: Bearer {access_token}
```

To create a user:

```
POST https://graph.microsoft.com/v1.0/users
Content-Type: application/json

{
  "accountEnabled": true,
  "displayName": "Jane Doe",
  "mailNickname": "janedoe",
  "userPrincipalName": "janedoe@yourtenant.onmicrosoft.com",
  "passwordProfile": {
    "forceChangePasswordNextSignIn": false,
    "password": "P@ssword123"
  }
}
```

Note: Ensure your app has the necessary permissions (e.g., `User.ReadWrite.All`).

Security Considerations

- Use CAPTCHA or reCAPTCHA to prevent bot sign-ups.
- Enforce strong password policies.
- Consider integrating Multi-Factor Authentication (MFA).
- Monitor sign-up and sign-in attempts with Application Insights.

Customizing the UI for Local Accounts

You can deeply customize the UI for local accounts by editing the HTML/CSS templates provided in the user flow customization settings.

Key areas for customization:

- Branding: logo, background, colors
- Text labels: input placeholders, button text
- Layout: rearrange fields, add help text

JavaScript can also be injected for additional logic, such as dynamic field validation or tracking user actions with analytics.

Best Practices

- Keep the sign-up form minimal: ask for the fewest fields possible.

- Use progressive profiling: collect additional info later.

- Always verify email or phone numbers before allowing account creation.

- Regularly audit and clean up inactive accounts.

Conclusion

Setting up built-in local accounts in Azure AD B2C provides a robust, scalable, and secure way to manage users without relying on external providers. It supports full customization, integrates easily with your frontend, and enables you to implement modern authentication patterns.

By leveraging the Azure portal and user flows, you can quickly get started, while advanced scenarios can be addressed through custom policies and REST API integration.

Integrating Social Identity Providers (Google, Facebook, Microsoft, etc.)

Azure AD B2C allows you to integrate a wide range of social identity providers, such as Google, Facebook, Microsoft, LinkedIn, Twitter, and Apple. This integration provides users with a seamless and familiar sign-in experience, often improving user adoption and reducing friction during registration. These providers can be configured individually and combined with local accounts and other custom identity providers in a single user flow or custom policy.

Social providers delegate authentication to a third party, which then returns tokens to Azure AD B2C. These tokens are used to create and manage user accounts within your tenant.

Benefits of Using Social Providers

- **Improved User Experience**: Users can sign in with accounts they already trust and use.

- **Reduced Support Overhead**: No password reset or account recovery flows to maintain for these users.

- **Federated Identity**: Azure AD B2C handles the connection between your application and the provider.

- **Enhanced Trust**: Social logins often provide verified email addresses, profile photos, and names.

Common Social Providers Supported

- **Google**

- **Facebook**

- **Microsoft** **Account** **(MSA)**

- **LinkedIn**

- **Apple**

- **GitHub** (via OIDC)

- **Twitter** (requires custom setup)

Each provider requires a slightly different setup and configuration process, but all follow the general pattern of app registration, secret management, and configuration within Azure AD B2C.

Prerequisites

- You must have an Azure AD B2C tenant set up.

- You should have admin access to the identity provider platform (e.g., Google Developer Console).

- You must have created at least one user flow or custom policy.

General Steps for Integration

1. Register your application with the identity provider.

2. Obtain the client ID and client secret.

3. Configure the provider in Azure AD B2C.

4. Add the provider to a user flow or custom policy.

5. Customize and test the user journey.

Google Identity Provider Integration

Step 1: Register on Google Developer Console

1. Go to https://console.developers.google.com/.

2. Create a new project.

3. Go to **OAuth consent screen** and configure the consent details.

4. Under **APIs & Services > Credentials**, click **+ Create Credentials > OAuth client ID**.

5. Choose **Web application**.

6. Add the following **Authorized redirect URI**:

```
https://<tenant-name>.b2clogin.com/<tenant-
name>.onmicrosoft.com/oauth2/authresp
```

Replace `<tenant-name>` with your actual Azure AD B2C tenant name.

7. Copy the **Client ID** and **Client Secret**.

Step 2: Configure Google in Azure AD B2C

1. Go to **Azure portal > Azure AD B2C > Identity providers**.

2. Click **+ New OpenID Connect provider** (or use built-in if available).

3. Select **Google** from the list.

4. Enter the following:

- **Name:** Google

- **Client ID:** From Google Developer Console

- **Client Secret:** From Google Developer Console

- **Discovery endpoint**: `https://accounts.google.com/.well-known/openid-configuration`

5. Save the provider.

Step 3: Add Google to User Flow

1. Go to **Azure AD B2C** > **User flows**.
2. Select the target user flow.
3. Under **Identity providers**, enable **Google**.
4. Save the changes.

Step 4: Test the Integration

1. Run the user flow.
2. Choose **Google** on the sign-in screen.
3. Sign in with a valid Google account.
4. You'll be redirected to the application with a token from Azure AD B2C.

Facebook Identity Provider Integration

Step 1: Register on Facebook for Developers

1. Go to https://developers.facebook.com/.
2. Create a new app.
3. Under **Add a Product**, select **Facebook Login**.
4. Go to **Facebook Login** > **Settings**.
5. Add **Valid OAuth Redirect URIs**:

```
https://<tenant-name>.b2clogin.com/<tenant-
name>.onmicrosoft.com/oauth2/authresp
```

6. Copy the **App ID** and **App Secret**.

Step 2: Configure Facebook in Azure AD B2C

1. Go to **Azure AD B2C > Identity providers**.

2. Click **+ New Facebook provider**.

3. Enter:

- **Name**: Facebook

- **App ID**: From Facebook

- **App Secret**: From Facebook

4. Save the provider.

Step 3: Add Facebook to User Flow

Follow the same steps as with Google.

Microsoft Account (MSA) Integration

Step 1: Register with Azure App Registration Portal

1. Go to https://portal.azure.com.

2. Navigate to **Azure Active Directory > App registrations**.

3. Register a new application.

4. Configure **Redirect URI** as before.

5. Get the **Application (client) ID** and **Client Secret**.

Step 2: Configure MSA in Azure AD B2C

1. Go to **Azure AD B2C > Identity providers**.

2. Choose **Microsoft Account**.

3. Input:

- **Client** **ID**

- **Client** **Secret**

- **Discovery** **endpoint**:
  `https://login.microsoftonline.com/consumers/v2.0/.well-known/openid-configuration`

Using Custom OIDC Providers

Some providers (e.g., GitHub, Auth0, Okta) support OpenID Connect. You can configure them in Azure AD B2C using a custom OIDC provider.

```
{
  "Name": "GitHubOIDC",
  "ClientId": "abc123",
  "ClientSecret": "xyz456",
  "MetadataUrl": "https://github.com/login/oauth/.well-known/openid-configuration",
  "ResponseType": "code",
  "Scope": "openid profile email"
}
```

1. Go to **Azure AD B2C > Identity providers > New OpenID Connect**.

2. Provide the client ID, secret, metadata URL, and other parameters.

3. Save and test as usual.

Identity Provider Claim Mapping

When a user signs in using a social provider, Azure AD B2C maps the external claims (email, name, etc.) to your directory's claim schema.

Example:

External Claim	Mapped Claim
email	emails
name	displayName
sub	identityProviderId
picture (optional)	profilePhoto

You can manage and customize these mappings in custom policies by editing the **ClaimsTransformation** section.

Combining Social and Local Accounts

You can allow users to sign up/sign in with either social accounts or local credentials in the same user flow.

To do this:

- In the **User Flow**, enable multiple identity providers.

- Customize the UI layout to show all sign-in options.

Azure AD B2C handles account linking automatically based on email or phone number. However, you may implement custom logic using RESTful API connectors if you require tighter control.

Security Considerations

- **Token Validation**: Always validate the ID token and access token on your backend.

- **Client Secret Protection**: Never expose client secrets on the frontend.

- **Minimal Scopes**: Only request the claims you actually need.

- **Revocation Handling**: Monitor sign-ins and revoke tokens if needed.

Troubleshooting Tips

- **Redirect URI Mismatch**: Double-check the URI registered with the provider matches exactly.

- **Invalid Client Secret**: Make sure you're using the correct secret and it's not expired.

- **Missing Scopes**: Some providers (like Facebook) require approval for certain scopes like `user_birthday` or `user_gender`.

- **Browser Cookies**: Some identity providers block third-party cookies—ensure your application supports first-party flows when embedding iframes.

Best Practices

- **Use standard providers whenever possible** to benefit from built-in support.

- **Display branded buttons** (e.g., "Continue with Google") to improve user experience.

- **Ensure graceful fallbacks** in case a provider is down.

- **Implement account recovery options** in case users lose access to their social accounts.

- **Log and monitor** identity provider usage via Application Insights for analytics and debugging.

Conclusion

Integrating social identity providers with Azure AD B2C provides a powerful, user-friendly authentication model for modern applications. It reduces barriers to entry, enhances security, and simplifies user management. Whether using built-in providers like Google and Facebook or custom OIDC integrations, Azure AD B2C's flexibility ensures a consistent and secure user journey.

By registering with providers, correctly setting up identity configurations, and thoroughly testing user flows, you can deliver a seamless, scalable login experience that enhances trust and reduces friction for your users.

Custom Identity Providers via OpenID Connect and SAML

Azure AD B2C provides robust support for integrating custom identity providers using OpenID Connect (OIDC) and SAML 2.0 protocols. This capability allows organizations to federate authentication with partners, third-party providers, or their internal systems—enabling advanced scenarios such as enterprise single sign-on (SSO), B2B identity federation, or hybrid identity ecosystems.

Custom identity provider integration is essential for use cases where standard social providers are insufficient, or when compliance or security demands dictate the use of trusted third-party systems or legacy SAML-based systems.

Use Cases for Custom Identity Providers

- **Enterprise B2B scenarios** where users authenticate through an external Active Directory Federation Services (ADFS) or other SAML-compliant IdP.

- **White-labeled applications** that support customer-specific authentication systems.

- **Integration with third-party identity services** such as Okta, Ping Identity, Auth0, or custom-built authentication systems.

- **Single sign-on across multiple platforms**, including legacy applications.

- **Government or healthcare apps** that must federate with secure SAML providers.

Supported Protocols

Azure AD B2C supports:

- **OpenID Connect (OIDC)**: A modern, RESTful identity layer on top of OAuth 2.0.

- **SAML 2.0**: An XML-based, older but widely adopted federation standard.

Depending on your identity provider's capabilities, you will choose one of these protocols. OIDC is preferred when both options are available due to its simplicity, RESTful nature, and better mobile compatibility.

OpenID Connect Provider Integration

Step 1: Register Your Application with the OIDC Provider

This typically involves:

- Creating an app entry on the provider's portal.

Defining a redirect URI:

bash

```
https://<tenant-name>.b2clogin.com/<tenant-
name>.onmicrosoft.com/oauth2/authresp
```

-
- Retrieving the **client ID**, **client secret**, and **OIDC discovery endpoint**.

Step 2: Configure the Identity Provider in Azure AD B2C

1. Go to **Azure AD B2C** > **Identity providers**.
2. Select **+ New OpenID Connect provider**.
3. Provide the following details:

- **Name**: A friendly name (e.g., OktaOIDC)
- **Client ID**: From the OIDC provider
- **Client Secret**: From the OIDC provider
- **Metadata URL** (OIDC Discovery endpoint): Usually ends with `/.well-known/openid-configuration`
- **Scope**: openid profile email
- **Response Type**: code

Example:

```
{
  "Name": "OktaOIDC",
  "ClientId": "abc123-client-id",
  "ClientSecret": "xyz456-client-secret",
  "MetadataUrl": "https://dev-123456.okta.com/.well-known/openid-
configuration",
  "ResponseType": "code",
  "Scope": "openid profile email"
```

}

4. Save   the   provider.

Step 3: Add to User Flows

1. Navigate   to   your   user   flow.

2. Under   **Identity   providers**,   enable   your   new   provider.

3. Save   and   run   the   user   flow.

Claims Mapping

Azure AD B2C automatically maps standard claims (e.g., email, name, sub) to internal claim names. You can override or transform claims using **custom policies** and **claims transformations**.

Example transformation XML:

```
<ClaimsTransformation                              Id="MapOidcClaims"
TransformationMethod="FormatString">
  <InputClaims>
    <InputClaim                        ClaimTypeReferenceId="email"
TransformationClaimType="inputClaim1" />
  </InputClaims>
  <InputParameters>
    <InputParameter Id="stringFormat" DataType="string" Value="oidc-
{0}" />
  </InputParameters>
  <OutputClaims>
    <OutputClaim                  ClaimTypeReferenceId="customOidcId"
TransformationClaimType="outputClaim" />
  </OutputClaims>
</ClaimsTransformation>
```

SAML 2.0 Identity Provider Integration

Step 1: Gather Required Metadata

You'll need:

- The **SAML metadata URL** or **XML file** from the identity provider.

- The **Issuer URI**.

- The **Single Sign-On (SSO) URL**.

- The **X.509 certificate** (Base64 encoded public key).

Step 2: Add a SAML Identity Provider in B2C

1. Go to **Azure AD B2C > Identity providers**.

2. Select **+ New SAML provider**.

3. Enter:

- **Name**: A unique name (e.g., PartnerSAML)

- **Metadata URL or XML**: Provided by the IdP

- **Reply URL**: Azure AD B2C will generate this for you

- **Issuer URI**: The entity ID of the IdP

4. Save the configuration.

Example SAML XML Snippet

```
<EntityDescriptor         entityID="https://saml.identity-provider.com/"
xmlns="urn:oasis:names:tc:SAML:2.0:metadata">
  <IDPSSODescriptor
protocolSupportEnumeration="urn:oasis:names:tc:SAML:2.0:protocol">
    <KeyDescriptor use="signing">
      <KeyInfo xmlns="http://www.w3.org/2000/09/xmldsig#">
        <X509Data>
          <X509Certificate>MIID...AB</X509Certificate>
        </X509Data>
      </KeyInfo>
    </KeyDescriptor>
    <SingleSignOnService
Binding="urn:oasis:names:tc:SAML:2.0:bindings:HTTP-Redirect"
                    Location="https://sso.identity-
provider.com/login"/>
  </IDPSSODescriptor>
```

```
</EntityDescriptor>
```

Step 3: Configure Claims Mapping

SAML responses can contain various attribute names. You must map them to Azure AD B2C claims.

```
<ClaimType Id="email">
  <DisplayName>Email Address</DisplayName>
  <DataType>string</DataType>
  <DefaultPartnerClaimTypes>
    <Protocol                                    Name="SAML2"
PartnerClaimType="http://schemas.xmlsoap.org/ws/2005/05/identity/cla
ims/emailaddress" />
  </DefaultPartnerClaimTypes>
</ClaimType>
```

Use the `PartnerClaimType` node to define how external claim names are matched to internal ones.

Testing Custom Providers

To test your identity provider integration:

1. Run your user flow from Azure AD B2C.

2. Select your custom provider.

3. Complete the authentication steps.

4. Verify the returned claims in the ID token and Azure logs.

If you're using **custom policies**, you can log out claims using `<OutputClaim ClaimTypeReferenceId="email" />` and `<DisplayClaim>` to print them during the orchestration steps.

Troubleshooting Common Issues

Problem	Resolution
Invalid client secret	Double-check your secret and ensure it hasn't expired.
Redirect URI mismatch	Make sure the redirect URI is exactly as expected by the IdP.
Unsupported response type	Verify that your identity provider supports `code` or `id_token`.
Missing claims	Review the IdP claim configuration; some may require permission or consent.
SAML certificate validation failed	Ensure your certificate is properly formatted and current.

Advanced Scenarios

Multiple Identity Providers for Same Domain

In some B2B scenarios, you might want to route users from specific domains (e.g., @partner.com) to a custom IdP. This is possible using **custom policies** with **domain hints** and **claim resolvers**.

```
<OrchestrationStep        Order="1"       Type="CombinedSignInAndSignUp"
ContentDefinitionReferenceId="api.selfasserted">
  <ClaimsProviderSelections>
    <ClaimsProviderSelection TargetClaimsExchangeId="GoogleExchange"
/>
    <ClaimsProviderSelection TargetClaimsExchangeId="PartnerSAML" />
  </ClaimsProviderSelections>
</OrchestrationStep>
```

With a **custom JavaScript** on the login page, you can inspect the entered email and pre-select the correct IdP.

Account Linking

If a user signs in with a custom IdP but already has a local account with the same email, Azure AD B2C can link the accounts. This requires:

- A common identifier (email, username, etc.)
- A user journey that supports **lookup** **and** **link** logic
- REST API calls to query or create user records dynamically

Security Best Practices

- Always use **HTTPS endpoints** for metadata, SSO, and discovery URLs.
- Use **short-lived client secrets** and rotate them regularly.
- Minimize **scope** and requested claims to reduce data exposure.
- Validate the **audience (aud)** and **issuer (iss)** fields of tokens received from IdPs.
- Enable **token encryption** for SAML assertions if supported.
- Use **Application Insights** for monitoring and auditing federated sign-ins.

Conclusion

Custom identity provider integration in Azure AD B2C unlocks a wide range of possibilities for advanced authentication scenarios. Whether using OpenID Connect for modern, token-based identity systems or SAML for legacy enterprise systems, Azure AD B2C provides the flexibility and control needed to deliver secure, scalable, and user-friendly identity federation.

With proper planning, thorough testing, and strong security practices, custom identity providers can seamlessly fit into your authentication strategy—enabling you to build inclusive, global applications that meet complex user and partner needs.

Multi-Factor Authentication (MFA) Setup

Multi-Factor Authentication (MFA) is a critical security measure that adds an additional layer of protection beyond just a username and password. In Azure AD B2C, MFA ensures that even if credentials are compromised, an attacker would still need access to the second factor—typically a mobile device or authenticator app—to complete the sign-in process.

Azure AD B2C supports MFA via text messages (SMS) and mobile authenticator apps that generate Time-based One-Time Passwords (TOTP), such as Microsoft Authenticator or Google Authenticator. MFA can be enabled per user flow or through custom policies for more granular control, and it can also be enforced conditionally.

Why Use MFA in Azure AD B2C?

- **Enhanced Security**: Prevents unauthorized access due to credential theft.

- **Compliance**: Helps meet requirements like GDPR, HIPAA, and PCI-DSS.

- **User Trust**: Signals to users that their data is protected by modern security practices.

- **Phishing Resistance**: Reduces risk from common social engineering attacks.

MFA Delivery Methods Supported in B2C

- **SMS-based** **Verification** **Codes**

- **TOTP** **(Time-based** **One-Time** **Password)** **via** **Authenticator** **Apps**

Note: Azure AD B2C currently does not support push notifications or voice call verification.

Enabling MFA in User Flows

Step 1: Create or Edit a User Flow

1. Go to **Azure portal** > **Azure AD B2C** > **User flows**.

2. Select or create a **Sign up and sign in** or **Sign-in only** flow.

Step 2: Configure MFA

1. Under **Multi-Factor Authentication**, select **Enabled** or **Conditional**.

2. Choose the **verification methods** you want to allow:

   - SMS

   - Authenticator app (TOTP)

For best results, allow both to give users choice.

3. Save   the   user   flow.

Step 3: Test the User Flow

1. Run   the   user   flow.

2. Sign   in   with   a   test   user.

3. Azure   AD   B2C   will   prompt   for   MFA   depending   on   your   configuration.

MFA Configuration Modes

Azure AD B2C supports three configuration modes for MFA in built-in user flows:

- **Disabled**:   MFA   is   not   used.

- **Enabled**:   MFA   is   always   required.

- **Conditional**:   MFA   is   required   based   on   certain   criteria,   such   as:

    - First-time   sign-in

    - High-risk   country

    - IP   range   (via   custom   claims   and   policies)

    - Number   of   failed   attempts

Example of Conditional MFA with Built-in User Flow

Azure AD B2C allows basic conditional logic in built-in flows. For advanced scenarios (e.g., IP filtering), you need to use custom policies.

Custom MFA with Identity Experience Framework (IEF)

To implement advanced MFA logic using **custom policies**, you must define orchestration steps that invoke MFA when certain claims are true.

Sample TrustFrameworkExtensions.xml Snippet

```
<OrchestrationStep Order="3" Type="ClaimsExchange">
  <Preconditions>
```

```
<Precondition Type="ClaimEquals" ExecuteActionsIf="true">
  <Value>isMfaRequired</Value>
  <Value>true</Value>
  <Action>SkipThisOrchestrationStep</Action>
</Precondition>
</Preconditions>
<ClaimsExchanges>
  <ClaimsExchange                         Id="PhoneFactorExchange"
TechnicalProfileReferenceId="PhoneFactor-InputOrVerify" />
</ClaimsExchanges>
</OrchestrationStep>
```

This example invokes MFA only if the isMfaRequired claim is true. You can set that claim in earlier steps based on geography, device fingerprint, or user group membership.

TOTP-Based MFA via Authenticator Apps

Azure AD B2C supports TOTP-based apps like Microsoft Authenticator and Google Authenticator. To enable TOTP:

1. Ensure **TOTP** is allowed in your user flow or custom policy.

2. The user is prompted to scan a QR code during enrollment.

3. Once enrolled, users enter a rotating code from the app to complete authentication.

TOTP Enroll/Verify Custom Policy Flow

```
<TechnicalProfile Id="TOTP-InputOrVerify">
  <DisplayName>TOTP Verification</DisplayName>
  <Protocol Name="Proprietary" Handler="Web.TotpVerificationHandler"
/>
  <InputClaims>
    <InputClaim ClaimTypeReferenceId="email" />
  </InputClaims>
  <OutputClaims>
    <OutputClaim ClaimTypeReferenceId="authenticationSource" />
  </OutputClaims>
</TechnicalProfile>
```

Note: TOTP setup is not exposed via the portal UI; it must be configured in custom policies.

MFA Resilience and Fallback Strategies

MFA should not introduce significant friction or account lockouts. Consider:

- Allowing both SMS and TOTP, so users can switch if one fails.

- Providing a support link or fallback flow (e.g., email-based verification) in case MFA fails.

- Enabling device-based remember options to avoid repeated prompts.

Remember MFA for Trusted Devices

Azure AD B2C allows setting **persistent sessions** to avoid MFA prompts on trusted devices.

In **custom policies**, you can implement logic to skip MFA if a trust claim or cookie exists.

Example:

```
<Precondition Type="ClaimEquals" ExecuteActionsIf="true">
  <Value>deviceTrustLevel</Value>
  <Value>high</Value>
  <Action>SkipThisOrchestrationStep</Action>
</Precondition>
```

Security Considerations and Best Practices

- **Use MFA by Default**: Even for low-risk users. SMS alone is better than nothing.

- **Avoid SMS-only for High Security**: Use TOTP for sensitive data access.

- **Rotate TOTP Secrets Periodically**: Prompt users to re-enroll after 6–12 months.

- **Log and Monitor MFA Events**: Use Application Insights or Azure Monitor.

- **Lock Down MFA Registration**: Only allow during sign-up or via trusted profile edit flows.

- **Never Store MFA Secrets**: Azure handles this internally; do not attempt to replicate externally.

Auditing and Monitoring MFA Events

Azure AD B2C logs MFA events to **Azure Monitor**, **Log Analytics**, and **Application Insights** (if configured).

Key telemetry includes:

- MFA challenge issued
- MFA method selected
- MFA passed/failed
- MFA device used
- MFA enrollment initiated/completed

You can write custom KQL queries to analyze usage and detect anomalies.

Sample KQL Query

```
customEvents
| where name == "MFAChallengeIssued"
| summarize count() by tostring(customDimensions.method), bin(timestamp, 1d)
```

This shows daily counts of MFA challenges per method (SMS, TOTP, etc.).

Localization and UX Customization

All MFA prompts and instructions can be localized via **page layouts** (in user flows) or **content definitions** (in custom policies). Customize:

- SMS text message body
- Verification page instructions

- TOTP setup screens (including QR code instructions)

SMS Template Customization

1. Go to **Azure AD B2C** > **User flows** > **Language customization**.

2. Edit the **SMS verification** message to match your brand voice.

Example SMS:

```
[Contoso] Your security code is: 123456. Enter it to complete your
sign-in.
```

Limitations and Considerations

Feature	Supported
Push notification MFA	✗
Voice call MFA	✗
Email MFA	✗
SMS-based MFA	✓
TOTP-based MFA	✓
Custom MFA provider integration	✓ (via REST API connector)
Risk-based MFA enforcement	✓ (in custom policies)

To implement unsupported methods like email MFA, you would need to build a **RESTful API connector** that verifies a one-time code sent via email, and call it from your custom policy.

Advanced: REST API-Driven MFA

You can invoke external services to implement custom MFA mechanisms (e.g., hardware tokens, biometric verifications) using the **RESTful API Connector** feature.

Example:

```
<ClaimsExchange                                    Id="CustomMfaExchange"
TechnicalProfileReferenceId="REST-VerifyCustomMfa" />
```

Then, define `REST-VerifyCustomMfa` as a REST API call to your service. This allows integration with third-party identity protection systems or bespoke authentication logic.

Conclusion

Enabling MFA in Azure AD B2C is one of the most impactful ways to protect user accounts and elevate your application's security posture. Whether you opt for built-in user flows with SMS and TOTP support or leverage custom policies for fine-grained conditional logic and external provider integration, B2C gives you the flexibility and power to enforce strong authentication standards.

By balancing usability and security, customizing the experience to match your brand, and carefully monitoring MFA performance and telemetry, you can deliver a secure and seamless experience for all users.

Chapter 4: User Flows and Custom Policies

Understanding User Flows (Built-in Policies)

Azure Active Directory B2C (Azure AD B2C) provides two primary mechanisms to define how users interact with your applications: **user flows** (also known as built-in policies) and **custom policies** (via the Identity Experience Framework). This section focuses on user flows—how they work, how to create and manage them, and when to use them in your identity management strategy.

User flows are predefined, configurable policies that cover common identity tasks such as sign-up, sign-in, profile editing, and password reset. They offer a streamlined path to implement user journeys without requiring you to write complex logic or XML definitions. This makes them especially appealing to teams looking to get up and running quickly with minimal overhead.

What is a User Flow?

A user flow is essentially a set of steps that users go through when interacting with your application. These steps may include:

- Choosing an identity provider (email, Google, Facebook, etc.)
- Signing up with user details
- Verifying an email address
- Setting a password
- Receiving a token upon successful authentication

User flows encapsulate all of this logic and present a pre-built UI hosted by Azure AD B2C. You can customize the appearance and behavior to a degree, but you're working within a defined framework that abstracts away most of the complexity.

Types of User Flows

Azure AD B2C offers several types of user flows depending on the task at hand:

- **Sign-up and sign-in:** A combined experience where users can either register a new account or sign in with an existing one.

- **Sign-up only:** Use this when you want to separate the registration process from sign-in.

- **Sign-in only:** Useful for returning users; no registration options are presented.

- **Profile editing:** Allows users to update their account information.

- **Password reset:** Enables users to recover access to their account if they've forgotten their password.

Each of these flows can be created and configured independently in the Azure Portal, and you can choose which applications each flow is associated with.

Creating a User Flow

To create a user flow:

1. Go to your **Azure AD B2C tenant** in the Azure portal.

2. Under **Policies,** select **User flows**.

3. Click **+ New user flow**.

4. Choose the flow type (e.g., **Sign up and sign in**).

5. Provide a name for the flow (e.g., B2C_1_SUSI).

6. Select the **identity providers** you want to support (e.g., Email, Facebook, Google).

7. Choose the **attributes** to collect and return (e.g., Display Name, Email, Object ID).

8. Click **Create**.

Once created, you can view, edit, and run the user flow directly from the portal.

Configuring User Attributes and Claims

Attributes are pieces of information about the user, such as their name, email, or job title. Claims are the values returned to the application in the token after the user completes the flow.

You can configure these in the **User attributes** section of a user flow. Here's how:

1. Open your user flow.

2. Click **User attributes**.

3. Select the attributes you want to:

   o Collect (ask the user to enter)

   o Return (include in the token)

For example, you might collect the user's given name and surname, and return these as claims to personalize the app experience.

Calling a User Flow from an Application

Each user flow has a unique endpoint URL that applications can redirect users to when initiating authentication. Here's a sample URL format:

```
https://<tenant-name>.b2clogin.com/<tenant-
name>.onmicrosoft.com/oauth2/v2.0/authorize?p=B2C_1_SUSI&client_id=<
client-
id>&nonce=defaultNonce&redirect_uri=https%3A%2F%2Fmyapp.com%2Fauth&s
cope=openid&response_type=id_token
```

In a Single Page Application (SPA) using MSAL.js, calling a user flow might look like this:

```
msalInstance.loginRedirect({
  scopes: ["openid"],
  authority:              "https://<tenant-name>.b2clogin.com/<tenant-
name>.onmicrosoft.com/B2C_1_SUSI"
});
```

This initiates the user flow for sign-up or sign-in. After the user completes the flow, an ID token is returned to the application.

Best Practices for Using User Flows

While user flows simplify identity management, it's important to follow best practices to ensure scalability, maintainability, and security:

- **Use descriptive names**: For example, `B2C_1_SignUpSignIn_WebApp` helps distinguish flows for different apps or use cases.

- **Reuse flows where appropriate**: Avoid creating unnecessary duplicates. One sign-in flow can be reused by multiple apps if configured properly.

- **Avoid sensitive operations with built-in flows**: For example, custom verification or business logic requiring REST API calls should use custom policies.

- **Plan for growth**: If you foresee the need for highly customized user journeys, consider using custom policies from the start.

Limitations of User Flows

Although user flows are powerful, they have limitations:

- **Limited customization**: HTML, CSS, and JavaScript customization is supported but constrained.

- **Fixed orchestration**: You can't change the step-by-step behavior beyond what's offered in the portal.

- **No conditional branching**: User flows lack the ability to dynamically alter flow logic based on user attributes or responses.

- **No external API calls**: You can't invoke REST APIs as part of the flow; that requires custom policies.

These limitations are intentional, as user flows are designed for simplicity and ease of use. For advanced requirements, transitioning to custom policies is often necessary.

Managing User Flows Across Environments

In real-world projects, you'll often have separate environments (Dev, Test, Prod). Unfortunately, user flows don't support export/import directly like custom policies. Instead, recreate them in each environment via the Azure portal or automate with PowerShell or Azure CLI.

Here's a simple example using PowerShell to create a user flow:

```
Connect-AzAccount
Select-AzSubscription -SubscriptionId "<your-subscription-id>"
New-AzADB2CUserFlow    -Name    "B2C_1_SignUpSignIn"    -UserFlowType
"SignUpOrSignIn"
```

Note: Always test user flows thoroughly in lower environments before deploying them to production.

User Flow vs. Custom Policy: When to Use What

Feature	User Flows	Custom Policies
Quick setup	✓	✗
Highly customizable UI	✗ (limited)	✓
External system integration	✗	✓
Conditional logic	✗	✓
REST API calls in flow	✗	✓
Ideal for MVPs and simple apps	✓	✗
Suitable for enterprise use cases	✗	✓

Summary

User flows in Azure AD B2C provide a fast, secure, and efficient way to enable common identity scenarios. Whether you're building a mobile app, web portal, or enterprise SaaS platform, user flows allow you to quickly integrate authentication without deep expertise in identity protocols.

While they may not support every customization need, user flows remain a vital tool in the Azure AD B2C toolbox—especially when time-to-market, ease of use, and security are top priorities.

By understanding their capabilities and constraints, and applying best practices in configuration and deployment, you can leverage user flows to deliver seamless and secure user experiences across your applications.

Creating and Managing Custom User Flows

In many scenarios, built-in user flows in Azure AD B2C provide sufficient flexibility to handle standard user journeys. However, for applications with more complex requirements—such as conditional logic, integration with external APIs, or identity transformation workflows—you'll often find the need to move beyond the limitations of built-in flows. Custom user flows, sometimes referred to interchangeably with custom policies, give developers complete control over the identity journey using the Identity Experience Framework (IEF).

This section explores how to plan, design, and implement custom user flows to support sophisticated identity experiences. We'll also cover the structure and composition of a custom policy, how to extend them using RESTful APIs, and how to manage them effectively across environments.

Understanding the Need for Custom User Flows

Custom user flows are essential when you need:

- Integration with third-party systems during authentication.

- Custom logic based on user attributes.

- Multiple-step verification processes.

- Dynamic behavior depending on user input.

- Custom token issuance rules and claims transformation.

Let's consider a few scenarios where custom user flows are preferable:

- A company wants users to verify a loyalty membership number against an internal API before completing sign-up.

- A healthcare portal must display different sign-in experiences based on the user's region.

- A multi-brand company wants one policy to handle all brand-specific sign-up flows, dynamically displaying appropriate branding.

Prerequisites for Working with Custom User Flows

Before creating custom policies, ensure you have the following:

1. **An** **Azure** **AD** **B2C** **tenant.**

2. **A global administrator account** or a user with sufficient privileges.

3. **Identity Experience Framework (IEF)** and **TrustFramework extensions** registered in your tenant.

4. **Azure AD B2C custom policy starter pack**, available from Microsoft's GitHub repository.

To register the required applications for custom policy execution, follow these steps:

1. Open your B2C tenant.

2. Register two applications: one for the Identity Experience Framework, and one for the Proxy Identity Experience Framework.

3. Configure API permissions and reply URLs as per Microsoft's documentation.

Structure of a Custom Policy

A custom policy is composed of several XML files, typically named:

- **TrustFrameworkBase.xml** – Base configuration provided by Microsoft, rarely modified.

- **TrustFrameworkExtensions.xml** – Your customizations and extensions go here.

- **SignUpOrSignin.xml, ProfileEdit.xml, PasswordReset.xml** – Policy definitions for specific user journeys.

Each XML file includes the following elements:

- **ClaimsSchema** – Defines what claims (user attributes) are in scope.

- **ClaimsTransformations** – Defines logic for manipulating claims.

- **TechnicalProfiles** – Connect to systems like Azure AD, REST APIs, or other identity providers.

- **OrchestrationSteps** – Describe the steps a user goes through during the policy.

Setting Up a Custom Sign-Up and Sign-In Flow

Download the Custom Policy Starter Pack

From GitHub:

bash

```
https://github.com/Azure-Samples/active-directory-b2c-custom-policy-
starterpack
```

1. Choose the "SocialAndLocalAccounts" folder if you want support for both email and social logins.

Modify **TrustFrameworkExtensions.xml**

Update tenant information in the file:

xml

```
<TrustFrameworkPolicy    xmlns:xsi="http://www.w3.org/2001/XMLSchema-
instance"
                    xmlns:xsd="http://www.w3.org/2001/XMLSchema"
                    PolicyId="B2C_1A_TrustFrameworkExtensions"
                    TenantId="yourtenant.onmicrosoft.com"

PublicPolicyUri="http://yourtenant.onmicrosoft.com/B2C_1A_TrustFrame
workExtensions">
```

2.

Customize **Claims** **and** **Steps**

Add a custom claim to the schema:

xml

```xml
<ClaimType Id="membershipNumber">
  <DisplayName>Membership Number</DisplayName>
  <DataType>string</DataType>
  <DefaultPartnerClaimTypes>
    <Protocol Name="OAuth2" PartnerClaimType="membershipNumber" />
  </DefaultPartnerClaimTypes>
  <UserHelpText>Enter your loyalty membership number</UserHelpText>
</ClaimType>
```

3.

Add **REST** **API** **Validation**

Use a TechnicalProfile to call an API that verifies the membership number:

xml

```xml
<TechnicalProfile Id="REST-ValidateMembership">
  <DisplayName>Validate Membership Number</DisplayName>
  <Protocol                                     Name="Proprietary"
Handler="Web.TPEngine.Providers.RestfulProvider, Web.TPEngine">
    <Metadata>
      <Item Key="ServiceUrl">https://api.example.com/validate</Item>
      <Item Key="SendClaimsIn">Body</Item>
    </Metadata>
    <InputClaims>
      <InputClaim ClaimTypeReferenceId="membershipNumber" />
    </InputClaims>
    <OutputClaims>
      <OutputClaim ClaimTypeReferenceId="isValidMembership" />
    </OutputClaims>
  </Protocol>
</TechnicalProfile>
```

4.

Add **to** **Orchestration** **Steps**

Define when the API call occurs:

xml

```xml
<OrchestrationStep Order="2" Type="ClaimsExchange">
```

```
<ClaimsExchanges>
  <ClaimsExchange                        Id="ValidateMembership"
TechnicalProfileReferenceId="REST-ValidateMembership" />
  </ClaimsExchanges>
</OrchestrationStep>
```

5.

Uploading Custom Policies

1. Navigate to the **Identity Experience Framework** blade in the Azure Portal.

2. Upload the policies in this order:

   o TrustFrameworkBase.xml

   o TrustFrameworkExtensions.xml

   o SignUpOrSignin.xml (or other journey files)

Use the portal's validation and error reporting features to troubleshoot any issues.

Testing and Debugging Custom Policies

To test a policy:

- Go to **Identity Experience Framework** > **Custom policies**
- Click the policy you want to test (e.g., `B2C_1A_SignUpOrSignIn`)
- Click **Run now**, and follow the authentication steps in the browser

Use Application Insights for deeper debugging. Enable it in your policy like so:

```
<Item Key="InstrumentationKey">your-app-insights-key</Item>
```

Monitor logs to capture policy execution, REST API results, and claim values.

Managing Policy Versions and Environments

Because custom policies are code (XML files), use a version control system such as Git to track changes. Maintain separate branches or folders for different environments (e.g., dev, test, prod).

For deployment, consider automating the upload process using PowerShell or Azure CLI. Here's a basic example in PowerShell:

```
Import-AzB2CPolicy  -PolicyId  "B2C_1A_SignUpOrSignIn"  -FilePath
"./SignUpOrSignin.xml"
```

Always test new policy versions in a development tenant before deploying to production.

Security and Performance Considerations

When extending user journeys with custom logic, security becomes critical:

- Use HTTPS for all REST API integrations.
- Validate all external input rigorously.
- Do not return sensitive data as claims unless necessary.
- Limit token size by only returning essential claims.

Performance can be impacted by API latency or complex orchestration. Optimize by:

- Using short orchestration chains.
- Minimizing external calls.
- Caching static data when possible.

Real-World Use Case: Enterprise Onboarding Flow

Imagine a B2B SaaS platform where:

- Admin users sign up using email and must verify their company domain.

- A backend system checks if the company exists or creates one if needed.

- The policy dynamically routes users to complete KYC checks before sign-in.

Such a journey would require:

- RESTful API integration for company checks.

- Conditional branching.

- Claims transformation to issue role-specific tokens.

Custom policies are essential for implementing such logic.

Summary

Custom user flows provide unparalleled flexibility for implementing complex, enterprise-grade identity experiences in Azure AD B2C. While they require a deeper learning curve and involve maintaining XML-based configuration, the payoff is full control over authentication, integration with external systems, and dynamic claim issuance.

By understanding the architecture of a custom policy, how to compose orchestration steps and technical profiles, and how to manage these policies across environments, you can build secure, scalable, and deeply integrated identity solutions tailored to your application's specific needs.

When built with care, tested thoroughly, and versioned properly, custom user flows unlock the full potential of Azure AD B2C for even the most demanding scenarios.

Introduction to Identity Experience Framework (IEF)

The Identity Experience Framework (IEF) is the engine that powers custom policies in Azure Active Directory B2C. It enables the full extensibility of user journeys by allowing developers to define every aspect of the authentication process using a declarative XML-based policy language. Unlike built-in user flows, which offer limited customization, IEF gives you complete control over orchestration steps, claims processing, third-party integrations, token issuance, and UI branding.

This section serves as a comprehensive guide to understanding what the Identity Experience Framework is, how it fits into the Azure AD B2C architecture, and how to leverage its capabilities to build robust, flexible, and secure identity solutions.

Core Concepts of the Identity Experience Framework

IEF is built on a modular system of policies and elements that control how identities are handled and presented. Here are some foundational concepts:

- **Claims**: Key-value pairs that represent information about a user (e.g., `email`, `displayName`, `roles`).

- **ClaimsSchema**: A schema that defines which claims exist and their data types.

- **ClaimsTransformation**: Logic that transforms one or more input claims into output claims, using functions such as string manipulation, comparison, or regex.

- **TechnicalProfile**: Represents a specific task in the journey—such as calling an identity provider, invoking a REST API, or issuing a token.

- **OrchestrationStep**: Describes a step in the user journey, such as collecting credentials or displaying a UI screen.

- **ContentDefinition**: Defines the HTML templates used during each orchestration step.

- **RelyingParty**: The policy file that ties everything together and serves as the entry point for a specific user journey.

How IEF Differs from Built-In User Flows

Feature	Built-In User Flows	Identity Experience Framework
Customization Level	Basic	Advanced
Conditional Logic	Not Supported	Fully Supported
REST API Integration	Not Supported	Fully Supported
Multi-Step and Complex Journeys	Not Supported	Fully Supported
UI Branding	Limited	Full Control
Claims Transformation	Minimal	Extensive

Use Cases	Standard Apps	Enterprise, Regulated Apps

IEF allows organizations with complex identity requirements to enforce business-specific logic during sign-in, sign-up, and other flows.

Anatomy of a Custom Policy in IEF

A full identity journey using IEF generally consists of four main policy files:

1. **TrustFrameworkBase.xml**
   Provided by Microsoft, serves as the foundational policy with default configurations.

2. **TrustFrameworkExtensions.xml**
   Contains custom claims, transformations, and technical profiles that extend the base policy.

3. **Journey-specific** policy
   Examples: `SignUpOrSignin.xml`, `ProfileEdit.xml`, `PasswordReset.xml`. These define orchestration steps and invoke logic defined in extensions.

4. **RelyingParty** policy
   The file exposed to applications for authentication. It references a specific journey defined above.

Each file references elements defined in others, forming a complete execution plan from user entry to token issuance.

Defining Custom Claims

Custom claims are defined in the `ClaimsSchema` section. Here's an example of a custom claim for storing a user's department:

```
<ClaimType Id="department">
  <DisplayName>Department</DisplayName>
  <DataType>string</DataType>
  <DefaultPartnerClaimTypes>
    <Protocol Name="OAuth2" PartnerClaimType="department" />
  </DefaultPartnerClaimTypes>
  <UserHelpText>Your department within the organization</UserHelpText>
```

```
</ClaimType>
```

This claim can now be collected during user registration, used in transformations, or returned in tokens.

Using Claims Transformations

Claims transformations are rules applied to manipulate claim values. Common use cases include:

- Normalizing   case

- Concatenating   strings

- Comparing   values

- Assigning   default   values

Example: Assigning a default user role if none is provided:

```
<ClaimsTransformation                              Id="AddDefaultUserRole"
TransformationMethod="FormatStringClaim">
  <InputClaims />
  <InputParameters>
    <InputParameter Id="stringFormat">User</InputParameter>
  </InputParameters>
  <OutputClaims>
    <OutputClaim                              ClaimTypeReferenceId="role"
TransformationClaimType="createdClaim" />
  </OutputClaims>
</ClaimsTransformation>
```

You can chain multiple transformations together in a step or use them inline within TechnicalProfiles.

Understanding Technical Profiles

A TechnicalProfile performs a specific operation. Key types include:

- **Self-Asserted**: Displays a form to collect user input.

- **Azure Active Directory**: Authenticates against Azure AD.

- **REST API**: Calls an external service.

- **JWT Issuer**: Issues a token to the application.

Example: A Self-Asserted TechnicalProfile to collect user data:

```
<TechnicalProfile Id="SelfAsserted-UserRegistration">
  <DisplayName>User registration</DisplayName>
  <Protocol                                      Name="Proprietary"
Handler="Web.TPEngine.Providers.SelfAssertedAttributeProvider">
    <Metadata>
      <Item
Key="ContentDefinitionReferenceId">api.selfasserted</Item>
    </Metadata>
    <InputClaims />
    <OutputClaims>
      <OutputClaim ClaimTypeReferenceId="email" Required="true" />
      <OutputClaim  ClaimTypeReferenceId="givenName"  Required="true"
/>
    </OutputClaims>
    <UseTechnicalProfileForSessionManagement    ReferenceId="SM-Noop"
/>
  </Protocol>
</TechnicalProfile>
```

This profile is often the first step in the journey and can include UI customization through Content Definitions.

Building a Complete Orchestration Flow

OrchestrationSteps define the sequence of steps in the user journey. Each step may collect input, invoke logic, or issue tokens.

Example of a 4-step orchestration:

```
<OrchestrationSteps>
```

```
<OrchestrationStep Order="1" Type="ClaimsExchange">
  <ClaimsExchanges>
    <ClaimsExchange                     Id="UserRegistrationExchange"
TechnicalProfileReferenceId="SelfAsserted-UserRegistration" />
  </ClaimsExchanges>
</OrchestrationStep>
<OrchestrationStep Order="2" Type="ClaimsExchange">
  <ClaimsExchanges>
    <ClaimsExchange                         Id="ValidateUserInput"
TechnicalProfileReferenceId="REST-ValidateUser" />
  </ClaimsExchanges>
</OrchestrationStep>
<OrchestrationStep          Order="3"            Type="SendClaims"
CpimIssuerTechnicalProfileReferenceId="JwtIssuer" />
</OrchestrationSteps>
```

Each step transitions the user forward through the journey. Steps can include validation, data enrichment, or conditional redirection.

Integrating External Systems

IEF makes it possible to integrate external systems via REST APIs. This allows real-time validation or enrichment of user data.

Example use cases:

- Verify email domains against a whitelist
- Look up CRM records
- Validate government-issued IDs
- Enforce business logic through custom rules engines

Here's a TechnicalProfile calling a REST API:

```
<TechnicalProfile Id="REST-CheckDomain">
  <DisplayName>Check Email Domain</DisplayName>
  <Protocol                                    Name="Proprietary"
Handler="Web.TPEngine.Providers.RestfulProvider, Web.TPEngine">
    <Metadata>
```

```
        <Item              Key="ServiceUrl">https://api.contoso.com/check-
domain</Item>
      <Item Key="AuthenticationType">None</Item>
      <Item Key="SendClaimsIn">Body</Item>
    </Metadata>
    <InputClaims>
      <InputClaim ClaimTypeReferenceId="email" />
    </InputClaims>
    <OutputClaims>
      <OutputClaim ClaimTypeReferenceId="isApprovedDomain" />
    </OutputClaims>
  </Protocol>
</TechnicalProfile>
```

The result (isApprovedDomain) can determine the next step or block sign-up if invalid.

UI Customization and Branding

IEF policies reference HTML content through ContentDefinition elements. You can override these templates to fully control the look and feel of each screen in the journey.

Example:

```
<ContentDefinition Id="api.selfasserted">
  <LoadUri>https://yourcdn.com/custom_ui/selfasserted.html</LoadUri>
  <RecoveryUri>~/common/default_page_error.html</RecoveryUri>

<DataUri>urn:com:microsoft:aad:b2c:elements:contract:selfasserted:1.
2.0</DataUri>
</ContentDefinition>
```

This allows complete branding alignment with your corporate identity, support for custom fonts, layouts, logos, accessibility features, and multilingual content.

Token Customization and Claim Issuance

IEF lets you define precisely what claims are included in the tokens returned to the application. This is done through the OutputClaims element in the RelyingParty file.

Example:

```
<OutputClaims>
  <OutputClaim ClaimTypeReferenceId="email" />
  <OutputClaim ClaimTypeReferenceId="givenName" />
  <OutputClaim ClaimTypeReferenceId="role" />
</OutputClaims>
```

You can include custom roles, IDs, user types, or anything required by the application to enforce authorization.

Managing Policies and Scaling

Best practices for managing IEF policies in real-world environments include:

- **Version control**: Use Git for tracking and reviewing changes.

- **Environments**: Maintain separate versions for dev/test/prod.

- **Automation**: Deploy using PowerShell or CI/CD pipelines.

- **Monitoring**: Enable Application Insights to track usage and errors.

- **Security**: Always use secure endpoints, validate inputs, and audit changes regularly.

Here's a PowerShell snippet to automate uploads:

```
$policies  =  @("TrustFrameworkBase",  "TrustFrameworkExtensions",
"SignUpOrSignin")
foreach ($policy in $policies) {
    Import-AzB2CPolicy  -PolicyId  "B2C_1A_$policy"  -FilePath
"./$policy.xml"
}
```

Summary

The Identity Experience Framework is the foundation for building advanced identity workflows in Azure AD B2C. It provides a granular, powerful, and extensible model for defining every part of the user's identity journey—from login to claims issuance. Through its modular XML architecture, developers gain the ability to control UI screens, integrate with external systems, transform user data, and dynamically control flow logic.

While it introduces complexity compared to built-in flows, IEF is indispensable for organizations that need fine-tuned authentication mechanisms, third-party integrations, conditional user journeys, and enterprise-grade identity governance.

Mastering IEF unlocks the full potential of Azure AD B2C and positions your applications for scalable, secure, and highly personalized user experiences.

Writing and Deploying Custom Policies with XML

Writing and deploying custom policies using XML in Azure AD B2C involves working deeply with the Identity Experience Framework (IEF). This framework gives you complete control over how users authenticate, register, edit their profiles, and reset their passwords. It is an advanced feature of Azure AD B2C, intended for scenarios where built-in user flows do not offer enough flexibility.

Custom policies are written in XML and allow for complex orchestration steps, integration with external APIs, custom claims transformation, conditional logic, and personalized UI content. This section provides a comprehensive guide to authoring, structuring, and deploying these XML-based policies effectively and securely.

The Policy Hierarchy

Custom policies follow a layered structure composed of different policy files. Each policy serves a distinct role in the identity journey:

1. **TrustFrameworkBase.xml** – The foundational policy provided by Microsoft. This file should remain unchanged.

2. **TrustFrameworkExtensions.xml** – Your extension to the base policy. Most of your custom logic, claims, and technical profiles reside here.

3. **User Journey Policy** (e.g., `SignUpOrSignin.xml`, `ProfileEdit.xml`, `PasswordReset.xml`) – These files define the specific user flow and orchestration steps.

4. **RelyingParty Policy** – The entry point for the application. This policy references the user journey and specifies which claims are issued in the token.

Each of these XML files must follow a strict schema. Elements within them are deeply interconnected, so a clear understanding of how they work together is essential.

Writing the TrustFrameworkExtensions.xml

This policy is where you define your custom claims, claims transformations, content definitions, and technical profiles. It typically looks like this:

```
<TrustFrameworkPolicy
  xmlns:xsi="http://www.w3.org/2001/XMLSchema-instance"
  xmlns:xsd="http://www.w3.org/2001/XMLSchema"
  PolicyId="B2C_1A_TrustFrameworkExtensions"
  TenantId="yourtenant.onmicrosoft.com"

PublicPolicyUri="http://yourtenant.onmicrosoft.com/B2C_1A_TrustFrame
workExtensions"
  BasePolicyId="B2C_1A_TrustFrameworkBase">
```

Here's a breakdown of core sections:

ClaimsSchema

This defines the claims (user attributes) your policy will use.

```
<ClaimType Id="userRole">
  <DisplayName>User Role</DisplayName>
  <DataType>string</DataType>
  <DefaultPartnerClaimTypes>
    <Protocol Name="OAuth2" PartnerClaimType="role" />
  </DefaultPartnerClaimTypes>
</ClaimType>
```

ClaimsTransformations

Use these to manipulate or compute values from existing claims.

```
<ClaimsTransformation                            Id="AssignDefaultRole"
TransformationMethod="FormatStringClaim">
  <InputParameters>
    <InputParameter Id="stringFormat">User</InputParameter>
  </InputParameters>
  <OutputClaims>
```

```
      <OutputClaim                          ClaimTypeReferenceId="userRole"
TransformationClaimType="createdClaim" />
  </OutputClaims>
</ClaimsTransformation>
```

TechnicalProfiles

These are the functional units of the policy. Each TechnicalProfile performs a task like collecting input, authenticating, or calling a REST API.

```
<TechnicalProfile Id="SelfAsserted-Registration">
  <DisplayName>Registration</DisplayName>
  <Protocol                                      Name="Proprietary"
Handler="Web.TPEngine.Providers.SelfAssertedAttributeProvider">
    <Metadata>
      <Item
Key="ContentDefinitionReferenceId">api.selfasserted</Item>
    </Metadata>
    <OutputClaims>
      <OutputClaim ClaimTypeReferenceId="email" Required="true" />
      <OutputClaim ClaimTypeReferenceId="userRole" />
    </OutputClaims>
  </Protocol>
</TechnicalProfile>
```

Creating the User Journey

The user journey defines the flow a user will go through. It's made up of orchestration steps, each invoking a technical profile.

```
<UserJourney Id="SignUpOrSignIn">
  <OrchestrationSteps>
    <OrchestrationStep Order="1" Type="CombinedSignInAndSignUp">
      <ClaimsProviderSelections>
        <ClaimsProviderSelection
ValidationClaimsExchangeId="LocalAccountSigninEmail" />
      </ClaimsProviderSelections>
      <ClaimsExchanges>
```

```
        <ClaimsExchange                        Id="LocalAccountSigninEmail"
TechnicalProfileReferenceId="SelfAsserted-Registration" />
      </ClaimsExchanges>
    </OrchestrationStep>

    <OrchestrationStep Order="2" Type="ClaimsExchange">
      <ClaimsExchanges>
        <ClaimsExchange                               Id="IssueToken"
TechnicalProfileReferenceId="JwtIssuer" />
      </ClaimsExchanges>
    </OrchestrationStep>
  </OrchestrationSteps>
</UserJourney>
```

Writing the RelyingParty Policy

This is the entry point for your application and must be explicitly linked in the application settings. The RelyingParty file references the user journey, defines the token claims, and ties everything together.

```
<TrustFrameworkPolicy
  PolicyId="B2C_1A_SignUpOrSignIn"
  TenantId="yourtenant.onmicrosoft.com"

PublicPolicyUri="http://yourtenant.onmicrosoft.com/B2C_1A_SignUpOrSi
gnIn"
  xmlns:xsi="http://www.w3.org/2001/XMLSchema-instance"
  xmlns:xsd="http://www.w3.org/2001/XMLSchema"
  BasePolicyId="B2C_1A_TrustFrameworkExtensions">
  <RelyingParty>
    <DefaultUserJourney ReferenceId="SignUpOrSignIn" />
    <TechnicalProfile Id="JwtIssuer">
      <OutputClaims>
        <OutputClaim ClaimTypeReferenceId="email" />
        <OutputClaim ClaimTypeReferenceId="userRole" />
      </OutputClaims>
    </TechnicalProfile>
  </RelyingParty>
</TrustFrameworkPolicy>
```

UI Customization via Content Definitions

To customize the UI, you'll use `ContentDefinition` elements pointing to HTML templates or CDN-hosted pages.

```
<ContentDefinition Id="api.selfasserted">
  <LoadUri>https://cdn.example.com/selfasserted.html</LoadUri>
  <RecoveryUri>~/common/default_page_error.html</RecoveryUri>

<DataUri>urn:com:microsoft:aad:b2c:elements:contract:selfasserted:1.
2.0</DataUri>
</ContentDefinition>
```

This gives you full control over layout, branding, custom fields, localization, and accessibility.

Deploying Custom Policies

Once your XML files are written and validated locally, you need to upload them to your B2C tenant:

1. Go to **Azure Portal > Azure AD B2C > Identity Experience Framework**.

2. Upload the files in this order:

   - TrustFrameworkBase.xml (only once, provided by Microsoft)

   - TrustFrameworkExtensions.xml

   - User Journey Policies (e.g., SignUpOrSignin.xml)

   - RelyingParty (e.g., B2C_1A_SignUpOrSignIn.xml)

If there are errors, the portal will return validation messages pointing to the exact line and issue.

Automating Deployment with PowerShell

You can automate policy uploads using PowerShell:

```
$tenant = "yourtenant.onmicrosoft.com"
$policyFiles           =            @("TrustFrameworkExtensions.xml",
"SignUpOrSignin.xml", "B2C_1A_SignUpOrSignIn.xml")

foreach ($file in $policyFiles) {
  $policyId = (Get-Content $file -Raw) -match 'PolicyId="([^"]+)"' |
Out-Null; $matches[1]
    az ad b2c policy create --name $policyId --type "Custom" --file
$file
}
```

Integrating this script into a CI/CD pipeline ensures consistent deployment across development, staging, and production environments.

Testing and Troubleshooting

After deployment, test the custom policy by navigating to the policy under **Identity Experience Framework > Custom Policies**, clicking **Run now**, and selecting your application.

Debugging Tips:

- Use browser dev tools to inspect claims and error messages.

- Enable Application Insights for telemetry and failure tracing.

- Log inputs/outputs in your REST APIs to confirm integrations.

- Add debugging output claims in TechnicalProfiles to trace values.

Example output claim for debugging:

```
<OutputClaim                    ClaimTypeReferenceId="debugInfo"
AlwaysUseDefaultValue="true" DefaultValue="Checkpoint A reached" />
```

Best Practices

- **Keep policies modular**: Don't overload a single file—use extensions and reusable profiles.

- **Use versioning**: Name policies with version tags, e.g., `B2C_1A_SignUpOrSignIn_v2`.

- **Secure REST APIs**: Use tokens or IP restrictions to protect endpoints.

- **Avoid claim bloat**: Only return claims your app truly needs.

- **Validate XML with tools**: Use an XML linter or Visual Studio Code plugins.

- **Comment liberally**: Explain what each section does for future maintainers.

Migrating from Built-In User Flows

If you've previously used built-in user flows, the migration process involves:

1. Replicating existing logic in TechnicalProfiles and OrchestrationSteps.

2. Ensuring you collect and issue the same set of claims.

3. Replacing redirect URLs in your application to point to the custom policy endpoints.

Policy endpoint format:

```
https://<tenant>.b2clogin.com/<tenant>.onmicrosoft.com/oauth2/v2.0/a
uthorize?p=B2C_1A_SignUpOrSignIn&client_id=<id>&nonce=defaultNonce&r
edirect_uri=<url>&scope=openid&response_type=id_token
```

Summary

Writing and deploying custom policies with XML is a powerful yet intricate process that unlocks the full potential of Azure AD B2C. Through the Identity Experience Framework, you can define custom claims, authenticate through various identity providers, integrate with APIs, and control the entire user journey. Though the learning curve is steep, the flexibility gained allows you to address nearly any authentication or identity challenge.

By structuring your policies thoughtfully, automating deployments, validating thoroughly, and following best practices, you can build secure, scalable, and maintainable identity solutions tailored to your exact business requirements.

Chapter 5: Branding and UX Customization

Customizing HTML/CSS for User Journeys

When implementing Azure AD B2C in any production application, aligning the identity experience with your application's branding is vital to maintain a consistent user experience. Azure AD B2C allows for deep customization of the UI elements used in its user flows. This includes modifying HTML, CSS, and JavaScript to ensure the login, registration, password reset, and other pages reflect your brand's design system.

This section will explore the various customization capabilities available within Azure AD B2C, focusing on HTML and CSS, how to structure custom templates, where to host them, and how to ensure accessibility and responsiveness.

Understanding the Custom Page Content Model

Azure AD B2C user flows by default use a Microsoft-hosted UI. While it is functional, it is generic and lacks branding. By enabling "custom page content," you gain control over the full HTML structure.

A custom page comprises the following:

- **HTML structure** (required)

- **CSS styling** (optional, inline or external)

- **JavaScript enhancements** (discussed later in Section 5.2)

- **Placeholders and claims** (B2C-provided tokens to inject dynamic data)

The page must contain a `<div id="api"/>` element, where Azure AD B2C injects its user journey forms.

```
<!DOCTYPE html>
<html lang="en">
<head>
  <meta charset="UTF-8" />
  <meta name="viewport" content="width=device-width, initial-scale=1.0" />
  <title>Contoso Identity</title>
```

```
    <link rel="stylesheet" href="styles.css" />
  </head>
  <body>
    <header>
      <img src="logo.png" alt="Contoso Logo" />
      <h1>Sign in to Contoso</h1>
    </header>

    <main>
      <div id="api"></div>
    </main>

    <footer>
      <p>&copy; 2025 Contoso Ltd. All rights reserved.</p>
    </footer>
  </body>
</html>
```

Note: The `#api` div is **mandatory**—if omitted, the B2C page will fail to load correctly.

Hosting Custom HTML and CSS

Azure AD B2C does not host static files such as HTML, CSS, or JavaScript. You must host your custom page content externally. Suitable options include:

- **Azure Blob Storage with anonymous access**

- **Static website hosting services (e.g., GitHub Pages, Netlify)**

- **Your organization's web servers**

Example: Hosting in Azure Blob Storage

1. Create a new storage account with a container set to public access.

2. Upload your HTML and CSS files.

3. Copy the blob URL (e.g., `https://mybranding.blob.core.windows.net/templates/login.html`)

4. Use this URL when configuring the user flow in the Azure Portal.

Setting Up a User Flow with Custom HTML

To use your custom HTML in a user flow:

1. Go to **Azure Portal** > **Azure AD B2C** > **User Flows**

2. Select an existing flow or create a new one

3. Go to the **Page Layouts** section

4. Enable **Use custom page content**

5. Provide the URL to your hosted HTML file

After saving, when the flow is executed, B2C will load your page instead of the default Microsoft layout.

Styling Forms with CSS

The layout and form elements injected into the `#api` div can be styled with custom CSS. Azure AD B2C uses consistent element IDs and classes, which allows targeted styling.

Common IDs and classes include:

- `#email` – Input for email

- `#password` – Password input

- `.button` – Submit buttons

- `.error` – Error message containers

Example CSS for styling:

```
body {
  font-family: 'Segoe UI', sans-serif;
  background-color: #f9f9f9;
  margin: 0;
```

```
  padding: 0;
}

header {
  text-align: center;
  padding: 2rem;
  background-color: #004578;
  color: white;
}

#api {
  max-width: 400px;
  margin: 2rem auto;
  background: white;
  padding: 2rem;
  border-radius: 8px;
  box-shadow: 0 0 12px rgba(0, 0, 0, 0.1);
}

input[type="text"],
input[type="email"],
input[type="password"] {
  width: 100%;
  padding: 1rem;
  margin-bottom: 1rem;
  border: 1px solid #ccc;
  border-radius: 4px;
}

.button {
  display: block;
  width: 100%;
  padding: 1rem;
  background-color: #0078d4;
  color: white;
  border: none;
  border-radius: 4px;
  font-weight: bold;
  cursor: pointer;
}
```

```css
.button:hover {
  background-color: #005a9e;
}

.error {
  color: red;
  font-size: 0.9rem;
}
```

Responsive Design Considerations

Given that user journeys can be initiated from mobile or desktop apps, responsive design is essential. Use media queries to adjust layouts based on screen size.

```css
@media (max-width: 600px) {
  #api {
    margin: 1rem;
    padding: 1rem;
    box-shadow: none;
    border-radius: 0;
  }

  header h1 {
    font-size: 1.5rem;
  }
}
```

Using Dynamic Content with Claim Substitutions

Azure AD B2C allows injecting dynamic data using claim substitutions. For example:

```html
<h2>Welcome, {givenName}</h2>
```

The {givenName} placeholder will be replaced with the actual claim value during runtime.

Supported claims vary depending on the step in the user flow, but commonly include:

- `{email}`

- `{givenName}`

- `{surname}`

- `{signInName}`

These can be helpful for providing a personalized experience.

Best Practices for HTML/CSS Customization

1. **Keep** **It** **Lightweight**
Avoid bloated HTML or large external libraries (like jQuery or full Bootstrap) unless absolutely necessary.

2. **Test** **Across** **Devices**
Always verify your UI on desktop and mobile to ensure usability.

3. **Respect** **B2C** **Structure**
Do not interfere with elements inside `#api` using JavaScript in a destructive way (e.g., removing inputs).

4. **Accessibility** **First**
Ensure labels are associated with inputs, contrast ratios are adequate, and the layout supports screen readers.

5. **Version** **and** **Audit**
Store versions of your HTML/CSS in version control (like Git), and keep track of which version is linked to each flow.

Sample HTML + CSS Project Structure

```
/branding
├── login.html
├── register.html
├── passwordreset.html
├── styles.css
└── logo.png
```

Each file serves a specific user journey page. You can reuse `styles.css` and use the same structure with different headers or contextual messages.

Troubleshooting Custom Pages

If your custom page fails to load:

- Check browser console for CORS errors

- Ensure the file is publicly accessible (no authentication required)

- Make sure the `#api` div exists

- Confirm you've correctly configured the URL in the user flow settings

For advanced error diagnostics, refer to Application Insights integration in Chapter 8.

Conclusion

Customizing the HTML and CSS of your Azure AD B2C user journeys elevates the professionalism and cohesion of your application's identity experience. From aligning visual branding to improving responsiveness and accessibility, thoughtful custom design enhances trust and usability.

In the next section, we'll explore how JavaScript can further enhance your forms, validate input fields, and manipulate behavior within the identity journeys.

Using JavaScript for Form Enhancements

JavaScript allows developers to inject powerful, dynamic behaviors into Azure AD B2C user journeys, elevating the experience beyond static HTML and CSS. With JavaScript, you can validate input, manipulate DOM elements, display localized content, respond to events, and dynamically guide users through the flow — all while maintaining full control over branding and interaction.

This section explores how JavaScript can be effectively used to enhance B2C forms, including best practices, restrictions, and advanced use cases. You'll also learn how to structure JavaScript for maintainability and performance.

Where and How JavaScript is Loaded

JavaScript can be included either directly in your custom HTML template or referenced externally via a `<script src="..."></script>` tag. For modularity, it's recommended to host your JS separately, similar to how you'd host your HTML and CSS.

Example:

```
<script                          src="https://mycdn.com/scripts/form-
enhancements.js"></script>
```

Alternatively, inline:

```
<script>
  document.addEventListener('DOMContentLoaded', function () {
    // Code here
  });
</script>
```

Important: Ensure scripts are loaded **after** the DOM is ready and injected B2C elements (in `#api`) are available.

___

Form Field Manipulation

You can easily access and manipulate form elements rendered by B2C using standard DOM APIs or helper libraries. For example:

```
document.addEventListener('DOMContentLoaded', function () {
  const emailField = document.querySelector('#email');
  if (emailField) {
    emailField.setAttribute('placeholder',    'Enter    your    company
email');
    emailField.style.borderColor = '#0078D4';
  }
});
```

You can also add tooltips or helper text dynamically:

```
const helper = document.createElement('small');
```

```
helper.textContent = 'Use your work email (e.g., name@company.com)';
helper.style.display = 'block';
helper.style.marginTop = '5px';
emailField.parentNode.appendChild(helper);
```

Custom Client-Side Validation

While Azure AD B2C handles backend validation, client-side validation improves user experience by catching errors early.

For instance, validating a phone number field:

```
document.addEventListener('DOMContentLoaded', function () {
  const phoneInput = document.querySelector('#phone');
  const form = document.querySelector('form');

  if (phoneInput && form) {
    form.addEventListener('submit', function (e) {
      const value = phoneInput.value.trim();
      const isValid = /^\+?[0-9]{10,15}$/.test(value);
      if (!isValid) {
        e.preventDefault();
        alert('Please enter a valid phone number.');
        phoneInput.focus();
      }
    });
  }
});
```

Custom validation allows you to apply company-specific input rules, e.g., only accept corporate emails ending in @contoso.com.

Dynamic Field Display

In some flows, it's useful to show or hide fields based on other input values. JavaScript can conditionally control visibility.

```
const orgField = document.querySelector('#organization');
```

```
const positionField = document.querySelector('#position');

orgField.addEventListener('input', function () {
  if (orgField.value.toLowerCase() === 'contoso') {
    positionField.parentNode.style.display = 'block';
  } else {
    positionField.parentNode.style.display = 'none';
  }
});
```

This improves form usability and reduces cognitive load by hiding irrelevant options.

Enhancing Accessibility with ARIA

B2C does not include full ARIA support out of the box. JavaScript can enhance accessibility by assigning ARIA roles or attributes.

```
const alertBox = document.querySelector('.error');
if (alertBox) {
  alertBox.setAttribute('role', 'alert');
  alertBox.setAttribute('aria-live', 'assertive');
}
```

This ensures screen readers announce errors as they appear, helping visually impaired users navigate the journey effectively.

Tracking and Analytics

JavaScript provides a way to hook into page events and send tracking data to analytics platforms such as Google Analytics, Microsoft Clarity, or custom APIs.

Example: Tracking login start

```
window.dataLayer = window.dataLayer || [];
window.dataLayer.push({
  event: 'b2c-login-start',
  flow: 'SignInSignUp',
  timestamp: new Date().toISOString()
```

```
});
```

Example: Logging form submission to Application Insights

```
form.addEventListener('submit', function () {
  if (window.appInsights) {
    window.appInsights.trackEvent({ name: 'B2CFormSubmitted' });
  }
});
```

Note: Ensure any tracking complies with GDPR/CCPA policies.

Localized Content Display

If your B2C flow is multilingual, JavaScript can display localized messages or adjust layout depending on `ui_locales`.

Access the locale parameter:

```
const urlParams = new URLSearchParams(window.location.search);
const locale = urlParams.get('ui_locales') || 'en';

if (locale === 'fr') {
  document.querySelector('h1').textContent = 'Connexion à Contoso';
}
```

You can load locale files dynamically:

```
fetch(`/locales/${locale}.json`)
  .then(res => res.json())
  .then(data => {
    document.querySelector('#email-label').textContent        =
data.labels.email;
  });
```

Handling B2C Errors

JavaScript can also help highlight and handle server-side errors that are injected into the page as part of the HTML.

Check for error containers:

```
const errorContainer = document.querySelector('.error');
if                        (errorContainer               &&
errorContainer.textContent.includes('AADB2C90118')) {
  // Redirect to password reset
  window.location.href = '/passwordreset';
}
```

You can provide friendly error messages or automate redirection when certain errors occur.

Preventing Common Mistakes

1. Don't Remove Required Elements

Never delete or move elements rendered inside `#api`, such as `<form>`, input fields, or buttons. These are required for B2C to operate correctly.

2. Defer Script Execution

Always wrap scripts inside `DOMContentLoaded` or `window.onload` to ensure DOM is ready. B2C injects content asynchronously, and premature access may result in null references.

3. Avoid External Scripts from Untrusted Domains

Due to security risks, scripts should be hosted on domains you control and served over HTTPS.

Advanced Use Case: Conditional Prefill

Sometimes, you may want to prefill a field conditionally based on user behavior or query parameters.

```
const params = new URLSearchParams(window.location.search);
const emailHint = params.get('email_hint');
if (emailHint) {
  const emailInput = document.querySelector('#email');
```

```
  if (emailInput) {
    emailInput.value = emailHint;
  }
}
```

This is useful when deep linking from marketing campaigns or app flows that already know the user's email.

Advanced Use Case: Custom Form Submission

Although you can't override the full submission logic, you can intercept clicks to perform pre-submit validation or UX changes.

```
const button = document.querySelector('button[type="submit"]');
button.addEventListener('click', function () {
  button.disabled = true;
  button.textContent = 'Submitting...';
});
```

Ensure you handle edge cases where the form does not submit, so you can re-enable the button.

Maintaining Clean and Modular JavaScript

For scalability, structure your JavaScript as modules. For example:

```
(function () {
  const FormEnhancer = {
    init() {
      this.attachValidation();
      this.setupPrefill();
    },
    attachValidation() {
      // Validation logic here
    },
    setupPrefill() {
      // Prefill logic here
    }
```

```
  };

  document.addEventListener('DOMContentLoaded', () => {
    FormEnhancer.init();
  });
})();
```

This avoids polluting the global scope and keeps code organized.

Conclusion

JavaScript is a powerful tool for enriching Azure AD B2C user flows. From validating inputs and showing tooltips to personalizing the experience and tracking usage, dynamic scripts bridge the gap between static templates and real-world interactivity.

Used responsibly, JavaScript can significantly improve both usability and engagement — but always test thoroughly, respect accessibility standards, and follow security best practices.

In the following section, we'll dive into localization and multilingual support, detailing how to structure and deliver user journeys that adapt to diverse user languages and regions.

Localization and Multilingual Support

In today's global digital landscape, offering localized and multilingual support is not just a nice-to-have — it's essential. Users expect applications and services to communicate in their native languages, honor regional preferences, and reflect cultural nuances. Azure AD B2C provides comprehensive support for localization, empowering developers to deliver identity experiences tailored to diverse global audiences.

This section explores how to implement full localization in Azure AD B2C, covering everything from language selection to translation of custom HTML, error messages, and dynamic content. We'll examine built-in capabilities and custom approaches to ensure every user feels at home in your identity journey.

Overview of Localization in Azure AD B2C

Azure AD B2C supports localization in two main contexts:

1. **Built-in   user   flow   content   localization**

2. **Custom   HTML/CSS/JavaScript   localization**

Built-in content includes error messages, labels, and system-generated text. When using custom pages, the responsibility shifts to developers to provide localized equivalents.

The localization behavior is driven primarily by the `ui_locales` query string parameter, which determines the language code used for that session.

Language Selection Mechanisms

Azure AD B2C supports three primary ways to determine which language to use:

1. `ui_locales` Query Parameter

This is the most direct and preferred method for selecting a locale.

Example:

```
https://contoso.b2clogin.com/contoso.onmicrosoft.com/B2C_1_SignUp?ui
_locales=fr
```

This tells B2C to use French (`fr`) for the current session.

2. Browser Language Detection

If `ui_locales` is not set, B2C defaults to the browser's language preferences (Accept-Language header).

3. Custom Language Picker

You can build a custom language picker in your HTML and reload the page with the desired `ui_locales` parameter.

```
<select id="languagePicker">
  <option value="en">English</option>
  <option value="fr">Français</option>
  <option value="es">Español</option>
</select>

<script>

document.getElementById('languagePicker').addEventListener('change',
function () {
    const selectedLang = this.value;
```

```
  const url = new URL(window.location.href);
  url.searchParams.set('ui_locales', selectedLang);
  window.location.href = url.toString();
});
</script>
```

Configuring Localization in Built-In User Flows

Azure AD B2C supports more than 36 languages out of the box. You can customize the default content for each language via the Azure Portal.

Steps:

1. Go to **Azure AD B2C** > **User Flows**

2. Select a user flow (e.g., B2C_1_SignUp)

3. Click **Languages**

4. Click **Add language** (e.g., French)

5. Customize text strings for labels, error messages, buttons, etc.

You can provide values for every translatable key in each supported language. Changes take effect immediately after saving.

Custom Page Localization (HTML/CSS/JS)

When using custom pages, localization becomes a manual process. You need to deliver translated HTML content and manage dynamic behaviors with JavaScript.

A common approach is to store translations in external JSON files and use JavaScript to apply localized content based on `ui_locales`.

Directory structure:

```
/branding
 ├── login.html
 ├── locales/
 │   ├── en.json
```

```
|   |── fr.json
|   └── es.json
└── scripts/
    └── localization.js
```

Sample en.json:

```json
{
  "title": "Sign in to Contoso",
  "emailLabel": "Email Address",
  "passwordLabel": "Password",
  "submitButton": "Sign In"
}
```

Sample fr.json:

```json
{
  "title": "Se connecter à Contoso",
  "emailLabel": "Adresse e-mail",
  "passwordLabel": "Mot de passe",
  "submitButton": "Se connecter"
}
```

JavaScript loader:

```javascript
document.addEventListener('DOMContentLoaded', () => {
  const                    locale                    =                    new
URLSearchParams(window.location.search).get('ui_locales') || 'en';

  fetch(`./locales/${locale}.json`)
    .then(response => response.json())
    .then(strings => {
      document.querySelector('h1').textContent = strings.title;
      document.querySelector('label[for="email"]').textContent    =
strings.emailLabel;
      document.querySelector('label[for="password"]').textContent    =
strings.passwordLabel;
```

```
    document.querySelector('button[type="submit"]').textContent   =
strings.submitButton;
    });
});
```

Localizing Error Messages

Azure AD B2C returns standard error messages (like AADB2C90118) that can be localized using either built-in translations or custom logic.

When using custom pages, you can override or supplement the default error handling with JavaScript:

```
const errorText = document.querySelector('.error');
if (errorText && errorText.textContent.includes('AADB2C90091')) {
  errorText.textContent = (locale === 'fr')
    ? "Le mot de passe est trop faible."
    : "Password is too weak.";
}
```

To make this scalable, store translations in your JSON files and reference them instead of hardcoding.

Localization of Custom Fields and Claims

If you include custom attributes (like jobTitle or department), you'll also want their labels to be localized.

In your custom HTML:

```
<label for="extension_jobTitle" id="jobLabel">Job Title</label>
<input type="text" id="extension_jobTitle" name="extension_jobTitle"
/>
```

Then update via JavaScript:

```
document.getElementById('jobLabel').textContent            =
translations.jobTitle;
```

Ensure all such custom fields have corresponding entries in your JSON translation files.

Best Practices for Multilingual Support

1. **Use ISO 639-1 Codes:** Stick with standard language codes (e.g., en, fr, es, de) and avoid ambiguous or made-up codes.

2. **Include a Default Fallback:** Always provide a fallback (typically English) in case a specific locale file is missing.

3. **Centralize Translations:** Use centralized JSON files for easy updates and consistent localization.

4. **Be Aware of Text Expansion:** Some languages require more space (e.g., German or Russian), so avoid fixed-width layouts.

5. **Handle Right-to-Left (RTL) Languages:** For Arabic (ar) or Hebrew (he), set dir="rtl" on the <html> tag and use appropriate styling.

```
<html lang="ar" dir="rtl">
```

6. **Include Language Testing in QA:** Localization testing should be part of your test cycle. Validate layout, translations, and UX across all supported locales.

Language-Specific CSS

Sometimes language-specific styling is needed to accommodate different text directions or font preferences.

```
html[lang="ar"] {
  font-family: 'Noto Naskh Arabic', serif;
  direction: rtl;
}

html[lang="ja"] {
  font-family: 'Yu Gothic', sans-serif;
```

```
}
```

Add this dynamically:

```
document.documentElement.setAttribute('lang', locale);
if (locale === 'ar' || locale === 'he') {
  document.documentElement.setAttribute('dir', 'rtl');
}
```

Testing Localization

Use the Azure AD B2C preview features to simulate different language settings without changing your browser locale.

Alternatively, construct deep links for each supported language:

```
https://contoso.b2clogin.com/contoso.onmicrosoft.com/B2C_1_SignIn?ui
_locales=de
```

Open each URL in a private browsing session and validate:

- Labels and buttons
- Error messages
- Field names and help text
- Content spacing and layout

Conclusion

Localization and multilingual support in Azure AD B2C unlock your application's potential for global reach. Whether leveraging built-in language features or building custom, dynamic translations with JavaScript, the tools are there to create inclusive and accessible identity journeys for users around the world.

From right-to-left language support to dynamic translations based on user context, Azure AD B2C offers the flexibility you need to serve users in their own language, building trust and satisfaction along the way.

In the next section, we'll explore accessibility and UX best practices to ensure every user, regardless of ability, can use your identity flows seamlessly.

Accessibility and UX Best Practices

Designing Azure AD B2C user journeys isn't just about branding and functionality — it's about building an inclusive experience for **everyone**. Accessibility (a11y) ensures that users with disabilities can interact with your application without barriers. Combined with solid UX (user experience) principles, you can make your identity flows not only compliant but intuitive and enjoyable for all users.

This section provides a deep dive into best practices for accessibility and UX within Azure AD B2C, particularly when using custom HTML, CSS, and JavaScript. From semantic markup to ARIA roles, keyboard navigation, and screen reader support, we'll explore practical steps to make your user journeys universally usable.

Why Accessibility Matters

Accessibility is more than just compliance with standards like WCAG (Web Content Accessibility Guidelines) or Section 508. It's about:

- Ensuring users with **visual, auditory, motor, or cognitive impairments** can interact with your application

- Supporting assistive technologies like **screen readers**, **screen magnifiers**, **voice input**, and **switch devices**

- Providing equal opportunity and **avoiding legal risks**

It also improves UX for **all users**. Well-structured, accessible interfaces tend to be cleaner, more consistent, and easier to use.

Semantic HTML: Foundation of Accessibility

Using the right HTML elements is the first step toward accessible design. Avoid generic `<div>` and `<span>` tags where more meaningful elements exist.

Use:

- `<form>` for the entire input area

- `<label>` for associating text with form fields

- `<fieldset>` and `<legend>` for grouped inputs
- `<button>` over `<a>` or `<div>` for actions

Example:

```
<form>
  <label for="email">Email Address</label>
  <input type="email" id="email" name="email" required aria-required="true" />

  <label for="password">Password</label>
  <input type="password" id="password" name="password" required aria-required="true" />

  <button type="submit">Sign In</button>
</form>
```

Semantic structure enables screen readers to understand and describe the page correctly.

Labels and Input Associations

Labels are vital for screen readers and users with cognitive difficulties. Every `<input>` should have a corresponding `<label>` with a matching `for` attribute.

Avoid using placeholders as a substitute for labels — they disappear when users type and are not always accessible.

Do:

```
<label for="username">Username</label>
<input id="username" name="username" type="text" />
```

Don't:

```
<input placeholder="Username" />
```

ARIA Roles and Attributes

The ARIA (Accessible Rich Internet Applications) specification fills in gaps for assistive technologies when native HTML isn't enough.

Use ARIA **to enhance**, not replace, semantic HTML.

Common roles and attributes:

- `role="alert"`: for dynamic error messages

- `aria-live="polite"` or `aria-live="assertive"`: for announcements

- `aria-describedby`: links inputs to additional context or help

- `aria-disabled`: for elements that look interactive but are disabled

Example:

```
<div class="error" role="alert" aria-live="assertive">
  Invalid email address.
</div>
```

Keyboard Navigation

Many users rely on a keyboard (or keyboard-emulating device) to navigate. Ensure:

- All interactive elements are reachable using the `Tab` key

- Focus order follows a logical path

- `Enter` or `Space` triggers button actions

- Custom controls support arrow keys or other expected behavior

Avoid custom elements that don't natively support keyboard interaction (e.g., `<div>` pretending to be a button).

To make a custom button accessible:

```
<div     role="button"     tabindex="0"     onclick="submitForm()"
onkeydown="if(event.key==='Enter') submitForm();">
  Sign In
</div>
```

But even better: just use a `<button>`.

Color Contrast and Visual Clarity

Color contrast ensures text is readable by users with low vision or color blindness. WCAG 2.1 requires a contrast ratio of:

- **4.5:1** for normal text

- **3:1** for large text (18pt or 14pt bold)

Use tools like **WebAIM Contrast Checker** to validate your color schemes.

Avoid using **color alone** to convey information:

Bad:

```
<span style="color: red;">Error: Required field</span>
```

Better:

```
<div class="error" role="alert">
  <strong>Error:</strong> Required field
</div>
```

Provide icons, underlines, or text labels in addition to color cues.

Focus Management and Visual Indicators

Focus indicators show users where they are on the page. Never remove outlines unless you provide a clear alternative.

Avoid:

```
button:focus {
  outline: none;
}
```

Instead:

```
button:focus {
  outline: 3px solid #005A9E;
  outline-offset: 2px;
}
```

If you use JavaScript to show or hide modal dialogs or error messages, make sure to shift focus appropriately:

```
document.getElementById('errorMessage').focus();
```

You can also use `tabindex="-1"` to programmatically focus non-interactive elements.

Responsive and Scalable Layouts

Accessible UX isn't just about disabilities — it's also about adapting to different screen sizes and devices.

Best Practices:

- Use **relative units** (em, rem, %) instead of fixed pixels
- Allow zooming (don't disable pinch-to-zoom on mobile)
- Design for **mobile-first**, then scale up
- Test with screen orientation changes

```
html {
  font-size: 100%;
}
```

```
@media (max-width: 600px) {
  .form-container {
    padding: 1rem;
  }
}
```

Error Handling and Validation

Clear, accessible error messages are critical to form usability.

- Display errors **next** **to** **the** **relevant** **field**
- Use clear, specific language
- Link error messages to fields using aria-describedby

Example:

```
<label for="email">Email</label>
<input id="email" aria-describedby="emailError" />
<div id="emailError" class="error" role="alert">
  Please enter a valid email address.
</div>
```

JavaScript should validate fields in real time or before submission and focus on the first error.

Accessible Loading and Feedback States

When a form is processing, users need feedback:

- Use a **loading** **spinner** or status message
- Set aria-busy="true" on the form or section
- Update aria-live regions when loading is complete

Example:

```
<div id="status" aria-live="polite">Signing you in...</div>
<form aria-busy="true">
  ...
</form>
```

Disable the submit button during processing:

```
submitBtn.disabled = true;
submitBtn.textContent = 'Submitting...';
```

Avoiding Timeouts and Surprises

Accessibility also includes being **predictable**. Warn users if the session will timeout or redirect unexpectedly.

For example, provide a countdown and allow extension:

```
<div id="timeoutWarning" role="alert" aria-live="assertive">
  Your session will expire in <span id="countdown">30</span> seconds.
  <button onclick="extendSession()">Continue</button>
</div>
```

Testing Accessibility

Use **manual testing** combined with tools:

- **Keyboard-only navigation:** Test entire flow without a mouse

- **Screen readers:** Use NVDA (Windows), VoiceOver (macOS), or TalkBack (Android)

- **Color blindness simulators:** Like Color Oracle

- **Automated tools:** Axe, Lighthouse, WAVE

But remember — **automated tests catch ~30%** of accessibility issues. Manual testing is essential.

UX Tips for Identity Journeys

Good UX complements accessibility. Consider these identity-specific best practices:

- **Minimize steps:** Keep sign-in and sign-up short

- **Clear CTAs:** Use descriptive button text like "Create Account" instead of "Next"

- **Progress indicators:** Show where users are in multi-step flows

- **Help links:** Provide "Forgot password?" and "Need help?" options clearly

- **Success feedback:** Show a confirmation or welcome message upon completion

---

Conclusion

Accessibility and UX in Azure AD B2C are not just about meeting checkboxes — they're about **respecting your users**, **removing friction**, and **delivering delight**. From semantic HTML to thoughtful error handling, color contrast to screen reader support, every decision you make in your custom pages influences the experience of someone with a unique need.

By following these best practices, you make your application better for **everyone**. And in the process, you demonstrate that your brand values inclusivity, usability, and excellence.

With branding, JavaScript enhancements, localization, and accessibility in place, you now have the tools to create a fully customized, world-class identity experience powered by Azure AD B2C. In the next chapter, we'll shift gears into technical integration: registering applications, acquiring tokens, and configuring backend APIs for secure authentication.

Chapter 6: API Integration and Application Configuration

Registering Applications in Azure AD B2C

To integrate your applications with Azure AD B2C, the first step is to register them within your B2C tenant. This process enables the applications to communicate securely with the B2C identity platform, acquire tokens for authentication and authorization, and integrate user flows or custom policies for user interaction.

The application registration process involves defining essential metadata such as redirect URIs, supported account types, scopes, and API permissions. Azure AD B2C treats each application as a "client" in the OAuth2/OpenID Connect flow, and registration is necessary for both frontend (SPA, mobile) and backend (web API, daemon) components.

Types of Applications

Azure AD B2C supports various application types:

- **Single-page applications (SPAs)** – JavaScript-based apps like those built with React, Angular, or Vue.

- **Mobile/native apps** – iOS and Android applications using MSAL or other OAuth2 libraries.

- **Web apps** – Server-side applications using libraries like ASP.NET, Node.js, or PHP.

- **Web APIs** – APIs protected by Azure AD B2C, validating tokens issued to clients.

- **Daemon apps** – Background services with client credentials flow, often used for backend automation.

Each of these applications has different configuration needs within the Azure portal.

Registering an Application

To register a new application in your Azure AD B2C tenant, follow these steps:

1. Sign in to the Azure Portal.

2. Navigate to **Azure AD B2C** > **App registrations**.

3. Click **+ New registration**.

4. Fill out the registration form:

- **Name**: A meaningful name, e.g., *MySPA*.

- **Supported account types**: Leave as default (only this organizational directory).

- **Redirect URI**: If registering a SPA, enter the URI where users will be redirected after authentication, e.g., `http://localhost:3000`.

- Choose **SPA** or **Web** depending on the application type.

5. Click **Register**.

After registration, you'll be taken to the app's overview page where you can copy the **Application (client) ID**—this is required in your application code.

Redirect URIs and Reply URLs

Redirect URIs (also known as reply URLs) are critical. They define where Azure AD B2C sends authentication responses. For SPAs, this might be:

```
http://localhost:3000
https://myapp.com/auth/callback
```

Ensure you include all valid redirect URIs under **Authentication** in your app registration. If you miss a URI, authentication will fail with an "unauthorized redirect" error.

Configuring Implicit vs Authorization Code Flow

Azure AD B2C recommends using the **authorization code flow with PKCE** (Proof Key for Code Exchange), especially for SPAs and mobile apps. This is more secure than the older implicit flow, which is no longer recommended.

To enable authorization code flow:

1. Go to the **Authentication** blade of your app registration.

2. Under **Platform configurations**, choose your platform (e.g., SPA).

3. Ensure **Authorization code (PKCE)** is selected.

4. Save the changes.

Exposing APIs to Clients

If you're building a protected web API, you'll also need to:

- Register the API as its own application.
- Define the scopes (permissions) the client app will request.
- Grant the client app access to those scopes.

Step-by-Step: Exposing an API

1. Register the API in **App registrations**.
2. Go to **Expose an API**.
3. Click **Set** for Application ID URI, e.g., `https://mytenant.onmicrosoft.com/myapi`.
4. Click **Add a scope**:
   - Scope name: `read`
   - Admin consent display name: `Read access to the API`
   - Admin consent description: `Allows reading data from the API`
   - Who can consent: Admins and users
   - Save.

Next, go to the client application's registration:

1. Go to **API permissions**.
2. Click **+ Add a permission** > **My APIs** > Select your API.
3. Choose the `read` scope you just defined.
4. Click **Add permissions**.
5. Click **Grant admin consent** for the tenant.

Configuring Application Secrets or Certificates

For confidential clients like web APIs or daemon apps, you must authenticate using a **client secret** or **certificate**.

Adding a Client Secret:

1. Navigate to your registered application.

2. Click **Certificates & secrets**.

3. Under **Client secrets**, click **+ New client secret**.

4. Provide a description and expiration period.

5. Click **Add** and copy the secret value immediately.

Note: Once you leave the page, you can't view the secret again.

Token Configuration

Azure AD B2C issues **ID tokens** and **access tokens** as per your app requirements. These can be configured under the **Token configuration** section in the app registration.

Adding Optional Claims:

1. Go to **Token configuration > + Add optional claim**.

2. Choose the token type (ID or access).

3. Select desired claims, such as `email`, `given_name`, `family_name`, etc.

4. Click **Add**.

This ensures your app receives necessary user information in the token.

Sample Configuration in Code (React App)

Here's a simple MSAL configuration for a SPA using the `@azure/msal-browser` library:

```
// src/authConfig.ts

export const msalConfig = {
  auth: {
    clientId: "YOUR_CLIENT_ID",
    authority:        "https://<tenant-name>.b2clogin.com/<tenant-name>.onmicrosoft.com/B2C_1_SIGNUP_SIGNIN",
```

```
    knownAuthorities: ["<tenant-name>.b2clogin.com"],
    redirectUri: "http://localhost:3000",
  },
  cache: {
    cacheLocation: "localStorage",
    storeAuthStateInCookie: false,
  }
};

export const loginRequest = {
  scopes: ["openid", "profile", "offline_access"]
};
```

In your React component, use MSAL hooks or context to trigger sign-in and token acquisition:

```
import { useMsal } from "@azure/msal-react";

const SignInButton = () => {
  const { instance } = useMsal();

  const handleLogin = () => {
    instance.loginRedirect(loginRequest);
  };

  return <button onClick={handleLogin}>Sign In</button>;
};
```

Handling Redirects

For SPAs, after login, the app should handle redirects to complete the login process:

```
import { PublicClientApplication } from "@azure/msal-browser";

const msalInstance = new PublicClientApplication(msalConfig);
msalInstance.handleRedirectPromise().then(response => {
  if (response) {
    // Handle signed-in user
    console.log("Access Token:", response.accessToken);
  }
```

```
});
```

Summary and Best Practices

- Always use **authorization code flow with PKCE** for SPAs and mobile apps.

- Store client secrets securely and rotate them periodically.

- Define only the necessary redirect URIs and scopes to reduce attack surface.

- Use **app roles and scopes** to enforce least privilege in backend APIs.

- Implement **token validation** on server-side APIs to protect resources.

- Use **tenant-specific authority URLs** to avoid phishing and misrouting.

In the next section, we'll look at how to acquire tokens and manage them within applications. Registering applications properly lays the foundation for secure, seamless identity integration across your ecosystem.

Acquiring Tokens (Access, ID, Refresh)

In Azure AD B2C, authentication and authorization are achieved through the issuance of security tokens: **ID tokens**, **access tokens**, and optionally, **refresh tokens**. These tokens serve different purposes and are essential for building secure and seamless user experiences in applications that consume Azure AD B2C services.

This section provides an in-depth look into how tokens are acquired, how they differ, how they are used in different application scenarios (SPA, mobile, web), and best practices around token management.

Token Types Overview

- **ID Token**: Contains identity information about the user. Primarily used by client applications to display user information or maintain a session.

- **Access Token**: Used to authorize access to a protected resource (e.g., API).

- **Refresh Token**: Used to acquire new access tokens and ID tokens without prompting the user to sign in again.

How Tokens Are Issued

Tokens are issued when an application performs a sign-in or token acquisition request using the **OAuth 2.0** and **OpenID Connect** protocols. The typical flows are:

- **Authorization Code Flow with PKCE** (Recommended for SPAs and mobile apps)

- **Client Credentials Flow** (For daemons and backend-to-backend services)

- **On-Behalf-Of Flow** (For middle-tier services acting on behalf of a user)

For interactive user flows, the **Authorization Code Flow with PKCE** is the most secure and standard approach, which can return all three tokens depending on configuration.

Token Acquisition Using MSAL

Microsoft Authentication Library (MSAL) simplifies token acquisition. Below is how MSAL handles the authorization code flow in a React SPA:

```
import { PublicClientApplication } from "@azure/msal-browser";
import { msalConfig, loginRequest } from "./authConfig";

const msalInstance = new PublicClientApplication(msalConfig);

// Redirect login
msalInstance.loginRedirect(loginRequest);

// After redirection
msalInstance.handleRedirectPromise().then(response => {
  if (response) {
    const idToken = response.idToken;
    const accessToken = response.accessToken;
    // use tokens
  }
});
```

Token Claims

Tokens are JSON Web Tokens (JWTs) and consist of **claims**, which are key-value pairs containing metadata such as:

- sub: Subject   (user   ID)

- email: User's   email   address

- name: Full   name   of   the   user

- aud: Audience   (client   ID   of   the   recipient)

- iss: Issuer   (Azure   AD   B2C   endpoint)

- exp: Expiration   time

- iat: Issued   at   time

You can view a decoded token at jwt.ms by pasting the token in.

Scopes and Resources

Tokens are tied to **scopes** and **resources**:

- When requesting a token, your app specifies the scopes it needs.

- The **resource** is the API for which the token is valid.

Example scope request:

```
scopes: ["https://<tenant>.onmicrosoft.com/api/read"]
```

If your app also wants the openid, profile, or offline_access scopes, include them as needed.

Requesting Tokens Silently

After the initial interactive sign-in, MSAL allows for **silent token acquisition**, which doesn't interrupt the user experience:

```
msalInstance.acquireTokenSilent(loginRequest).then(response => {
  console.log("Access token:", response.accessToken);
}).catch(error => {
  if (error instanceof InteractionRequiredAuthError) {
    return msalInstance.acquireTokenRedirect(loginRequest);
  }
});
```

This pattern is crucial for SPAs to refresh tokens without requiring user interaction.

Refresh Tokens

To support longer sessions, B2C issues refresh tokens when the `offline_access` scope is requested.

Key Points:

- ID token is short-lived (typically 1 hour).
- **Access token** is also short-lived.
- **Refresh token** is longer-lived (valid for days or weeks depending on policy).

Refresh tokens are used to obtain new ID/access tokens silently, especially in mobile or desktop apps:

```
msalInstance.acquireTokenSilent({
  scopes: ["openid", "profile", "offline_access"],
  account: msalInstance.getAllAccounts()[0]
});
```

Note: MSAL handles refresh token rotation internally.

Acquiring Tokens in Mobile Apps (React Native)

In mobile apps using `@azure/msal-react-native` or native libraries (iOS/Android), the token acquisition process is similar:

```
const result = await msalInstance.acquireToken({
  scopes: ["openid", "profile",
"https://<tenant>.onmicrosoft.com/api/read"]
});

console.log(result.accessToken);
```

Ensure your app is registered as a public client and uses a redirect URI like `msauth://<package-name>`.

Backend (Confidential Client) Token Flow

Backend services (e.g., Node.js APIs or background daemons) require the **client credentials flow**:

```
const formData = new URLSearchParams();
formData.append("grant_type", "client_credentials");
formData.append("client_id", "your-client-id");
formData.append("client_secret", "your-client-secret");
formData.append("scope",
"https://<tenant>.onmicrosoft.com/api/.default");

const              response              =              await
fetch("https://<tenant>.b2clogin.com/<tenant>.onmicrosoft.com/oauth2
/v2.0/token?p=B2C_1A_custom", {
  method: "POST",
  headers: { "Content-Type": "application/x-www-form-urlencoded" },
  body: formData.toString()
});

const tokenData = await response.json();
console.log(tokenData.access_token);
```

This flow does not involve user interaction and is suited for machine-to-machine scenarios.

Configuring User Flows to Return Tokens

To ensure your B2C user flows return the desired tokens:

1. Navigate   to   **User   flows**   >   Select   a   flow.

2. Click   **Application**   **claims**.

3. Choose   claims   to   include   in   the   **ID   token** and   **access   token**.

4. Save   changes.

Claims can include:

- email

- displayName

- custom   attributes

- extension_   fields   (from   custom   attributes)

Token Lifetimes and Expiration

By default, Azure AD B2C issues:

- **ID tokens** valid for 1 hour

- **Access tokens** valid for 1 hour

- **Refresh tokens** valid for 14 days (sliding expiration up to 90 days)

These can be adjusted using **Token Lifetimes** custom policies or by modifying the IEF XML policies.

Note: Token lifetimes configured via legacy methods are deprecated; use recommended Identity Experience Framework (IEF) methods.

Token Validation

APIs must validate access tokens before granting access:

- Validate **signature** using Microsoft public keys (available via metadata endpoint)

- Validate **aud**, **iss**, **exp**, and **sub** claims

- Reject expired or malformed tokens

Example using Node.js and jsonwebtoken:

```
const jwt = require('jsonwebtoken');
const jwksClient = require('jwks-rsa');

const client = jwksClient({
  jwksUri:
'https://<tenant>.b2clogin.com/<tenant>.onmicrosoft.com/discovery/v2
.0/keys?p=B2C_1A_signup_signin'
});

function getKey(header, callback) {
  client.getSigningKey(header.kid, function (err, key) {
    const signingKey = key.getPublicKey();
    callback(null, signingKey);
  });
}
```

```
jwt.verify(token, getKey, {
  audience: "your-api-client-id",
  issuer:
"https://<tenant>.b2clogin.com/<tenant>.onmicrosoft.com/v2.0/",
  algorithms: ['RS256']
}, function (err, decoded) {
  if (err) {
    console.log("Invalid token", err);
  } else {
    console.log("Token valid:", decoded);
  }
});
```

Common Errors and Troubleshooting

- **AADSTS7000215**: Invalid client secret.

- **AADSTS65001**: Consent required; admin must grant API permissions.

- **AADSTS50011**: Redirect URI mismatch.

- **token_renewal_error**: Often indicates stale sessions; perform logout and login again.

Security Recommendations

- Use **PKCE** for all public client flows.

- Avoid storing tokens in unsafe storage (e.g., localStorage in web apps).

- Rotate client secrets regularly.

- Use **HTTPS** for all redirect URIs and token endpoints.

- Use **scoped access tokens** instead of over-privileged tokens.

- Validate tokens in all backend APIs.

Conclusion

Acquiring and managing tokens in Azure AD B2C is foundational for secure application development. From initial interactive login to silent renewals and backend service authentication, understanding how each token works and fits into the broader identity lifecycle allows you to build applications that are secure, scalable, and user-friendly.

In the next section, we'll cover how to integrate tokens into SPAs for full authentication flows, managing sessions, and securing API calls end-to-end.

Integrating with Single-Page Applications (SPAs)

Single-Page Applications (SPAs) present unique challenges and opportunities when integrating with Azure AD B2C. These applications are often built using frameworks like React, Angular, Vue, or Svelte and run entirely in the browser. This means they cannot securely store secrets and must rely on secure authentication patterns, primarily the Authorization Code Flow with Proof Key for Code Exchange (PKCE).

In this section, we'll explore how to properly integrate SPAs with Azure AD B2C, using the Microsoft Authentication Library (MSAL), managing tokens, handling sessions, calling protected APIs, and implementing logout correctly.

Why Authorization Code Flow with PKCE?

The implicit flow was previously used in SPAs, but due to security limitations—such as the inability to refresh tokens securely and increased susceptibility to token theft—it has been deprecated. Azure AD B2C recommends using **Authorization Code Flow with PKCE** for all SPAs.

PKCE enhances security by eliminating the need for a client secret and mitigating interception of authorization codes.

Basic Flow for SPA Authentication

Here's how the flow works in a SPA with Azure AD B2C:

1. **User initiates login**.

2. **Authorization request** is sent to B2C.

3. **B2C authenticates the user** and redirects back with an authorization code.

4. The SPA **exchanges the code for tokens** (ID, access).

5. The SPA **stores tokens in memory or secure storage** (e.g., sessionStorage).

6. Tokens are used to **access protected APIs**.

7. Optionally, a **refresh token** is issued to silently renew tokens.

8. On logout, **tokens are cleared** and the user is redirected to a post-logout URI.

MSAL Configuration for a React App

Install the MSAL browser package:

```
npm install @azure/msal-browser @azure/msal-react
```

Create a configuration file:

```typescript
// authConfig.ts
export const msalConfig = {
  auth: {
    clientId: "YOUR_CLIENT_ID",
    authority:
"https://<tenant>.b2clogin.com/<tenant>.onmicrosoft.com/B2C_1A_SIGNI
N_SIGNUP",
    knownAuthorities: ["<tenant>.b2clogin.com"],
    redirectUri: "http://localhost:3000",
    postLogoutRedirectUri: "http://localhost:3000",
  },
  cache: {
    cacheLocation: "sessionStorage", // or localStorage
    storeAuthStateInCookie: false,
  }
};

export const loginRequest = {
  scopes:        ["openid",       "profile",       "offline_access",
"https://<tenant>.onmicrosoft.com/api/read"]
};
```

Set up the provider in your app:

```typescript
import { MsalProvider } from "@azure/msal-react";
import { PublicClientApplication } from "@azure/msal-browser";
import { msalConfig } from "./authConfig";

const msalInstance = new PublicClientApplication(msalConfig);

function App() {
```

```
  return (
    <MsalProvider instance={msalInstance}>
      <YourAppComponents />
    </MsalProvider>
  );
}
```

Logging In

Use MSAL hooks to initiate login:

```
import { useMsal } from "@azure/msal-react";

function SignInButton() {
  const { instance } = useMsal();

  const handleLogin = () => {
    instance.loginRedirect(loginRequest);
  };

  return <button onClick={handleLogin}>Sign In</button>;
}
```

Alternatively, `loginPopup()` can be used:

```
instance.loginPopup(loginRequest).then(response => {
  console.log("Login successful", response.account);
});
```

Handling Login Response

After redirection, the SPA must complete the login process:

```
useEffect(() => {
  instance.handleRedirectPromise().then(response => {
    if (response) {
      console.log("Tokens received", response);
    }
```

```
  });
}, []);
```

Getting Tokens for API Calls

Once signed in, get the access token silently:

```
const account = instance.getAllAccounts()[0];

instance.acquireTokenSilent({
  ...loginRequest,
  account
}).then(response => {
  const accessToken = response.accessToken;
  fetch("https://api.myapp.com/protected", {
    headers: {
      Authorization: `Bearer ${accessToken}`
    }
  });
});
```

Logging Out

Log the user out and redirect to the home page:

```
instance.logoutRedirect();
```

Or log out via popup:

```
instance.logoutPopup();
```

Make sure the `postLogoutRedirectUri` is correctly set in both the MSAL config and the app registration in the Azure portal.

Token and Session Management

SPAs must manage tokens carefully:

- Store tokens in `sessionStorage` or `memory` (preferable to localStorage due to XSS risk).

- Use `acquireTokenSilent` before each sensitive API call.

- If `InteractionRequiredAuthError` is thrown, prompt re-authentication.

MSAL handles caching and expiration internally. However, you should implement fallback logic for failed silent renewals:

```
.catch(error => {
  if (error instanceof InteractionRequiredAuthError) {
    return instance.acquireTokenRedirect(loginRequest);
  }
});
```

Best Practices for Secure SPA Integration

- **Always use PKCE** and authorization code flow.

- **Never store tokens in plain localStorage**—use sessionStorage or in-memory cache.

- Enable **CORS** on your backend API to allow token-authenticated requests.

- Define and enforce **CORS origin policies** in your APIs.

- Validate the access token on the backend using JWT libraries (e.g., `jsonwebtoken`, `Microsoft.Identity.Web`).

- **Avoid hardcoding tenant names or client IDs**—use environment variables.

- Use `navigateToLoginRequestUrl: false` to control post-login navigation.

- If you use multiple user flows (e.g., profile edit, password reset), ensure MSAL is correctly configured to handle each.

Handling Password Reset and Profile Edit

Azure AD B2C can be configured with multiple policies:

- Sign up/sign in: `B2C_1A_SIGNUP_SIGNIN`

- Password   reset: B2C_1A_PASSWORD_RESET

- Profile   edit: B2C_1A_PROFILE_EDIT

To redirect to a different flow:

```
const resetPasswordConfig = {
  ...msalConfig,
  auth: {
    ...msalConfig.auth,
    authority:
"https://<tenant>.b2clogin.com/<tenant>.onmicrosoft.com/B2C_1A_PASSW
ORD_RESET"
  }
};

instance.loginRedirect({
  ...loginRequest,
  authority: resetPasswordConfig.auth.authority
});
```

You can detect that a user is attempting a password reset via error codes:

```
.catch(error => {
  if (error.errorMessage.includes("AADB2C90118")) {
    // Trigger password reset flow
  }
});
```

Protecting Routes with MSAL

In React, you can create a ProtectedRoute component:

```
import { useIsAuthenticated } from "@azure/msal-react";
import { Navigate } from "react-router-dom";

const ProtectedRoute = ({ children }) => {
  const isAuthenticated = useIsAuthenticated();
```

```
    return isAuthenticated ? children : <Navigate to="/login" />;
};
```

Integrating with Backend APIs

To secure calls to your API:

1. Register the API in Azure AD B2C.

2. Expose scopes like `api/read`, `api/write`.

3. Add those scopes to your SPA registration.

4. Include the scopes in `loginRequest`.

5. Validate tokens in your API.

Example fetch call from SPA:

```
fetch("https://myapi.com/userinfo", {
  headers: {
    Authorization: `Bearer ${accessToken}`
  }
});
```

Using MSAL Events for Session Awareness

MSAL provides event hooks to monitor session changes:

```
msalInstance.addEventCallback((event) => {
  if (event.eventType === "msal:loginSuccess") {
    console.log("User logged in", event.payload.account);
  }
});
```

You can use these events to update UI, trigger side effects, or log telemetry.

Conclusion

Integrating SPAs with Azure AD B2C using MSAL and the Authorization Code Flow with PKCE offers a secure, scalable, and flexible way to handle user authentication. By leveraging MSAL's robust capabilities, handling tokens correctly, protecting routes, and connecting to secure APIs, developers can create seamless user experiences with strong identity safeguards.

The next section will cover backend API protection and token validation strategies to ensure your SPAs can securely communicate with services using Azure AD B2C-issued tokens.

Backend API Protection and Token Validation

Securing backend APIs is a fundamental part of building a robust application with Azure AD B2C. Once a Single-Page Application (SPA) or mobile app acquires access tokens from Azure AD B2C, these tokens must be validated by the backend API before granting access to protected resources. This ensures only authorized users can interact with sensitive endpoints.

In this section, we'll cover how to protect your backend APIs using Azure AD B2C access tokens, configure scopes, perform token validation, enforce fine-grained authorization, handle token lifetimes, and build secure middle-tier services using the on-behalf-of (OBO) flow.

Understanding the Security Model

When a frontend application requests an access token from Azure AD B2C, it includes scopes representing the APIs it wants to access. Azure AD B2C issues a JWT access token with claims about the user, the application, and the permissions granted. The backend API must validate these claims to ensure the token is legitimate and that the user has the necessary permissions.

Key Components in Securing APIs

- **Access Tokens**: Issued by Azure AD B2C and sent in the `Authorization` header.

- **JWT Validation**: Ensures tokens are issued by a trusted authority, for the intended audience, and are not expired.

- **Scopes**: Defined in API app registration to control access to API endpoints.

- **App Roles and Claims**: Help determine fine-grained access and authorization policies.

- **On-Behalf-Of (OBO) Flow**: Enables middle-tier APIs to call downstream APIs on behalf of the signed-in user.

Step-by-Step API Protection Guide

1. Register Your API in Azure AD B2C

In the Azure portal:

1. Go to **Azure AD B2C** > **App registrations** > **+ New registration**.

2. Register your API as a **web** **application**.

3. Set the **Redirect URI** to a placeholder, such as `https://localhost` (not used for APIs).

4. Save and copy the **Application** **(client)** **ID**.

2. Define API Scopes

1. Go to your API registration > **Expose** **an** **API**.

2. Set an **Application** **ID** **URI** (e.g., `https://contoso.com/api`).

3. Click **Add** a **scope,** define:

   - **Scope** name: `read`

   - **Display** name: `Read` `access`

   - **Description**: `Allows` `reading` `protected` `resources`

4. Repeat to create scopes like `write,` `admin.`

3. Configure the Client App

In the client app registration:

1. Go to **API** **permissions** > **+** **Add** a **permission.**

2. Choose **My** **APIs,** select your API.

3. Select the appropriate scopes (e.g., `read).`

4. Click **Grant** **admin** **consent.**

Ensure your SPA or mobile app requests these scopes in its `loginRequest.`

4. Sending the Access Token to the API

From the frontend (React, Angular, etc.), include the access token in the `Authorization` header:

```
fetch("https://api.contoso.com/data", {
  headers: {
    Authorization: `Bearer ${accessToken}`
  }
});
```

On the backend, your API must extract this token and validate it before processing the request.

Validating Tokens in a Node.js API

Install dependencies:

```
npm install express jsonwebtoken jwks-rsa
```

Set up middleware to verify the token:

```
const jwt = require("jsonwebtoken");
const jwksClient = require("jwks-rsa");

const client = jwksClient({
  jwksUri:
"https://<tenant>.b2clogin.com/<tenant>.onmicrosoft.com/discovery/v2
.0/keys?p=B2C_1A_SIGNIN"
});

function getKey(header, callback) {
  client.getSigningKey(header.kid, function (err, key) {
    const signingKey = key.getPublicKey();
    callback(null, signingKey);
  });
}

function verifyToken(req, res, next) {
  const token = req.headers.authorization?.split(" ")[1];

  jwt.verify(token, getKey, {
    audience: "your-api-client-id",
```

```
    issuer:
"https://<tenant>.b2clogin.com/<tenant>.onmicrosoft.com/v2.0/",
    algorithms: ["RS256"]
  }, (err, decoded) => {
    if (err) {
      return res.status(401).json({ error: "Unauthorized" });
    }
    req.user = decoded;
    next();
  });
}
```

Apply the middleware to your routes:

```
app.get("/data", verifyToken, (req, res) => {
  res.json({ message: "Secure data", user: req.user });
});
```

Token Claims to Inspect

When decoding and verifying the JWT, inspect these claims:

- iss: Must match Azure AD B2C token issuer
- aud: Must match your API's client ID
- exp: Ensure token has not expired
- scp: The list of scopes granted
- sub: The unique user identifier
- email, name: Optional user profile data

Validating Tokens in ASP.NET Core API

Add packages:

```
dotnet add package Microsoft.Identity.Web
dotnet add package Microsoft.AspNetCore.Authentication.JwtBearer
```

Configure your `Startup.cs` or `Program.cs`:

```
builder.Services.AddAuthentication(JwtBearerDefaults.AuthenticationS
cheme)
    .AddMicrosoftIdentityWebApi(options =>
    {
        options.Audience = "your-api-client-id";
        options.MetadataAddress                                    =
"https://<tenant>.b2clogin.com/<tenant>.onmicrosoft.com/v2.0/.well-
known/openid-configuration?p=B2C_1A_SIGNIN";
    },
    options => { });

builder.Services.AddAuthorization();

app.UseAuthentication();
app.UseAuthorization();
```

Secure your controllers:

```
[Authorize]
[ApiController]
[Route("api/[controller]")]
public class DataController : ControllerBase
{
    [HttpGet]
    public IActionResult Get() => Ok(new { message = "Protected data"
});
}
```

Fine-Grained Authorization Using Scopes

Inside your middleware or controller, you can enforce access by checking for specific scopes:

Node.js:

```
if (!req.user.scp.includes("read")) {
  return res.status(403).json({ error: "Insufficient permissions" });
}
```

ASP.NET:

```
[Authorize(Policy = "ReadScope")]
public IActionResult GetData() => Ok();
```

Define policies in `Startup.cs`:

```
services.AddAuthorization(options =>
{
    options.AddPolicy("ReadScope", policy =>
        policy.RequireClaim("scp", "read"));
});
```

Using App Roles for RBAC

In addition to scopes, Azure AD B2C supports **app roles**:

1. Define roles in `manifest.json` of your app registration.

2. Assign users or groups to these roles.

3. Inspect the `roles` claim in the token.

Example role:

```
"appRoles": [
  {
    "id": "e7f0e69e-3f5b-4cb6-8246-b0cf5a8eafcc",
    "allowedMemberTypes": ["User"],
    "description": "Admin role for managing users",
    "displayName": "Admin",
    "isEnabled": true,
    "value": "Admin"
```

```
    }
]
```

Supporting On-Behalf-Of (OBO) Flow

Middle-tier APIs that call downstream APIs can use the **OBO flow** to obtain a new token on behalf of the user:

1. Accept the incoming access token from the client.

2. Request a new token from Azure AD B2C for the downstream API.

Example (Node.js using Axios):

```javascript
const axios = require("axios");

async function getTokenOnBehalfOf(userToken) {
  const data = new URLSearchParams({
    grant_type: "urn:ietf:params:oauth:grant-type:jwt-bearer",
    client_id: "mid-tier-api-client-id",
    client_secret: "client-secret",
    assertion: userToken,
    scope: "https://<tenant>.onmicrosoft.com/downstream-api/read",
    requested_token_use: "on_behalf_of"
  });

  const response = await axios.post(

"https://<tenant>.b2clogin.com/<tenant>.onmicrosoft.com/oauth2/v2.0/
token?p=B2C_1A_SIGNIN",
    data
  );

  return response.data.access_token;
}
```

Handling Expired or Invalid Tokens

APIs should gracefully handle these scenarios:

- **Token** **expired**: Return `401` `Unauthorized`

- **Invalid** **signature**: Return `403` `Forbidden`

- **Missing** **scope**: Return `403` `Forbidden`

- **Malformed** **token**: Return `400` `Bad` `Request`

Always log token validation failures and avoid revealing sensitive information in error messages.

CORS Configuration

Ensure your API supports **Cross-Origin Resource Sharing (CORS)** for frontend clients:

Node.js (Express):

```
const cors = require("cors");

app.use(cors({
  origin: ["http://localhost:3000"],
  credentials: true
}));
```

ASP.NET:

```
services.AddCors(options =>
{
    options.AddPolicy("AllowSPA", builder =>
        builder.WithOrigins("http://localhost:3000")
            .AllowAnyHeader()
            .AllowAnyMethod());
});
```

Apply the policy:

```
app.UseCors("AllowSPA");
```

Best Practices for API Protection

- **Always validate tokens** server-side.
- **Use HTTPS** for all API endpoints.
- **Log security-related events** (auth failures, unexpected claims).
- **Rotate signing keys** regularly.
- **Use scopes and app roles** for granular access control.
- **Don't trust client data**—enforce all checks on the server.
- **Use token expiration wisely** to balance security and usability.
- **Set appropriate CORS rules** to protect your API.

Conclusion

Protecting backend APIs with Azure AD B2C involves careful planning, secure token handling, and robust validation mechanisms. Whether you're building a microservice architecture or a traditional client-server app, properly integrating token-based security is non-negotiable. By enforcing authentication, validating JWTs, leveraging scopes and roles, and supporting the OBO flow, you ensure your APIs are both secure and scalable.

With your backend secured, your full-stack B2C-powered application can confidently serve users and services with modern identity assurance.

Chapter 7: Advanced Customization and Extension

Using RESTful API Connectors in User Flows

Azure AD B2C is a highly extensible identity platform, and one of the most powerful customization features it offers is the ability to call RESTful API connectors during user flows. This capability allows you to integrate with external systems to enrich, validate, or transform data before continuing the user journey. Whether you're validating a user against an internal database, applying additional business logic, or retrieving external claims, RESTful API connectors provide the flexibility to go beyond built-in functionality.

This section explores how RESTful API connectors work, their configuration, security, common use cases, error handling, and performance considerations.

Overview of RESTful API Connectors

A RESTful API connector in Azure AD B2C allows your user flow or custom policy to call out to an external REST API. These calls are made during the execution of a user journey, where the response from the API can influence the path or data of the journey.

REST API connectors can be used in built-in user flows (with limited configuration) and custom policies (for full control). They typically support GET and POST methods and use standard JSON payloads to pass and receive data.

Some use cases include:

- Verifying user eligibility from an external system before sign-up

- Retrieving additional claims (e.g., subscription level, role)

- Performing fraud detection checks

- Checking terms of service acceptance status

- Synchronizing user data across systems

Prerequisites

Before configuring REST API connectors, ensure the following:

- You have access to a publicly available HTTPS REST endpoint.

- The endpoint supports bearer token or certificate-based authentication.

- The API is capable of receiving and responding with JSON data.

- If using in custom policies, you are comfortable with editing XML.

You will also need an Azure AD B2C tenant and at least one user flow or custom policy set up.

Creating a RESTful API

Let's begin by creating a sample RESTful API that your user flow will call.

```
// Sample API written in ASP.NET Core
[ApiController]
[Route("api/user")]
public class UserValidationController : ControllerBase
{
    [HttpPost("validate")]
    public IActionResult Validate([FromBody] JObject userInput)
    {
        var email = userInput["email"]?.ToString();

        // Dummy validation logic
        if (email == "blocked@example.com")
        {
            return BadRequest(new
            {
                version = "1.0.0",
                status = 400,
                userMessage = "This email address is not allowed."
            });
        }

        return Ok(new
        {
            version = "1.0.0",
            action = "Continue",
            additionalData = new {
                userType = "Premium"
            }
        });
```

```
    }
}
```

This simple API checks the email address in the request body and rejects a known bad one. Otherwise, it returns a custom claim.

Registering the API in Azure AD B2C

1. Navigate to your Azure AD B2C tenant in the Azure Portal.

2. Under **Identity Experience Framework**, select **API connectors** (or "External Identity Providers" in older UI).

3. Click **+ New API connector**.

4. Provide:

   - **Name:** UserValidationAPI

   - **Endpoint URL:** `https://yourdomain.com/api/user/validate`

   - **Authentication:** None or Certificate (for production)

   - **Timeout:** 30 seconds

   - **Claims included in requests:** Select `email`, `displayName`, etc.

Save the connector.

Configuring User Flows to Call the API

To use the API connector in a user flow:

1. Go to **User flows** and select a flow (e.g., `B2C_1_SignUpSignIn`).

2. Choose **API connectors** from the left menu.

3. Under **Before creating the user** or **After collecting attributes**, click **Add**.

4. Select the previously created API connector.

5. Map   input   and   output   claims.

Once added, this API will be invoked during the user flow based on the trigger point selected.

Using REST API in Custom Policies

Using the Identity Experience Framework (IEF), RESTful API connectors become even more powerful.

Here's a simplified example of calling an external API during a sign-up journey.

Define the technical profile for the API call:

```
<TechnicalProfile Id="REST-UserValidation">
  <DisplayName>User Validation API</DisplayName>
  <Protocol                                    Name="Proprietary"
Handler="Web.TPEngine.Providers.RestfulProvider, Web.TPEngine">
    <Metadata>
      <Item
Key="ServiceUrl">https://yourdomain.com/api/user/validate</Item>
      <Item Key="SendClaimsIn">Body</Item>
      <Item Key="AuthenticationType">None</Item>
    </Metadata>
    <InputClaims>
      <InputClaim ClaimTypeReferenceId="email" />
    </InputClaims>
    <OutputClaims>
      <OutputClaim ClaimTypeReferenceId="userType" />
    </OutputClaims>
    <UseTechnicalProfileForSessionManagement    ReferenceId="SM-Noop"
/>
  </Protocol>
</TechnicalProfile>
```

This profile posts the email claim to the API and expects a userType in return.

Add it to the orchestration step:

```
<OrchestrationStep Order="2" Type="ClaimsExchange">
  <ClaimsExchanges>
```

```
    <ClaimsExchange                          Id="Invoke-UserValidation"
TechnicalProfileReferenceId="REST-UserValidation" />
  </ClaimsExchanges>
</OrchestrationStep>
```

Now, your custom policy flow includes an external API check during execution.

Response Format and Error Handling

Azure AD B2C expects a specific response format from your API:

Successful response:

```
{
  "version": "1.0.0",
  "action": "Continue",
  "userType": "Premium"
}
```

Error response:

```
{
  "version": "1.0.0",
  "status": 400,
  "userMessage": "Email not allowed."
}
```

You can return ValidationError or ShowBlockPage as action values in custom policies to control flow behavior.

Authentication Options

Azure AD B2C supports several authentication modes when calling external APIs:

- **None**: Used in development or for public endpoints.
- **Basic Authentication**: Use with a username and password.

- **Client Certificate**: The most secure and recommended for production.

- **Managed Identity**: If hosted in Azure.

Configure the authentication method in the API connector's metadata or when setting up in the portal.

Performance Considerations

Since API connectors are invoked synchronously during user flow execution, their performance directly impacts the user experience. Keep in mind:

- **Latency**: Keep the round-trip time below 200ms.

- **Timeouts**: APIs that exceed the timeout period will fail the flow.

- **Scalability**: Your API must scale to handle peak login/registration traffic.

- **Error resilience**: Ensure graceful error handling and informative responses.

Use caching, request throttling, and asynchronous validation where possible to reduce load.

Logging and Troubleshooting

To debug RESTful API connector issues:

1. Enable **Application Insights** in your B2C tenant.

2. Monitor the **Trace logs** and **Exception logs** for failed connector calls.

3. Use **Postman** or **curl** to manually test your API with sample payloads.

4. Check **API response formats** to ensure they meet the expected schema.

Example test payload:

```
{
  "email": "test@example.com"
}
```

Best Practices

- Always validate input server-side.

- Return minimal data in the response—only what is required.

- Use HTTPS and secure authentication mechanisms.

- Include versioning in your API URL or payloads.

- Avoid calling APIs for optional features unless strictly needed.

- Monitor and log API performance and failures.

Summary

RESTful API connectors significantly extend Azure AD B2C's capabilities by enabling real-time integration with external systems during user flows. Whether you're adding dynamic claims, performing custom validations, or integrating with third-party services, this feature brings enterprise-level flexibility to your identity workflows.

Understanding how to configure, secure, and troubleshoot API connectors ensures that your solution is both robust and scalable. When used effectively, RESTful APIs allow Azure AD B2C to become the central hub in your authentication and user management strategy.

Integrating External Claims Sources

Integrating external claims sources in Azure AD B2C enables you to enrich your user profiles and authentication processes with data stored in other systems, such as CRMs, ERPs, subscription platforms, or internal databases. These sources can provide information like user roles, loyalty tiers, consent flags, or account restrictions. By embedding this dynamic data into your policies or user flows, you can create highly tailored and secure user journeys.

In this section, we will explore the different approaches to integrating external claims sources using custom policies, REST API connectors, and hybrid methods. We'll walk through real-world use cases, example technical profiles, response handling, and best practices for managing data flow securely and efficiently.

Why Integrate External Claims?

External claims integration solves several key challenges:

- **Personalized User Experiences**: Show personalized content or options during sign-in based on external attributes (e.g., `membershipLevel`, `preferredLanguage`, `accountStatus`).

- **Policy Enforcement**: Prevent access based on dynamic attributes (e.g., expired subscription, unpaid invoice, banned user).

- **Compliance**: Integrate consent flags or region-specific compliance requirements.

- **Data Synchronization**: Keep identity-related data consistent across systems in real time.

Azure AD B2C does not maintain complex business logic or external data. That logic must reside in external services that are queried as needed.

Approaches to External Claims Integration

There are several ways to bring in external claims:

1. **RESTful API Connector**
   Call a remote service via HTTP during a user flow or custom policy.

2. **Azure Functions or Logic Apps**
   Use these to orchestrate data access and return claims to B2C.

3. **Claims Mapping via Identity Providers**
   Retrieve claims directly from federated IdPs (e.g., Google, ADFS).

4. **Custom Extensions with Event Grids or Queues**
   Use event-based approaches to sync external data pre/post authentication.

The most common and flexible approach is using RESTful API connectors within the Identity Experience Framework (IEF).

Sample Scenario: Enriching Sign-In with CRM Data

Let's say you have a CRM system that stores a `loyaltyStatus` attribute for each user. When a user signs in, you want to retrieve this status and include it in the token.

Step 1: Define the Custom Claim

In your `TrustFrameworkExtensions.xml`, define the custom claim type:

```xml
<ClaimType Id="loyaltyStatus">
  <DisplayName>Loyalty Status</DisplayName>
  <DataType>string</DataType>
  <DefaultPartnerClaimTypes>
    <Protocol Name="OAuth2" PartnerClaimType="loyalty_status" />
  </DefaultPartnerClaimTypes>
  <UserHelpText>Status of user's loyalty program.</UserHelpText>
</ClaimType>
```

This ensures Azure AD B2C understands the structure and purpose of the new claim.

Step 2: Create REST API Connector Technical Profile

Add a technical profile that calls the external CRM service:

```xml
<TechnicalProfile Id="REST-GetCRMData">
  <DisplayName>Retrieve CRM Data</DisplayName>
  <Protocol                                        Name="Proprietary"
Handler="Web.TPEngine.Providers.RestfulProvider, Web.TPEngine">
    <Metadata>
      <Item
Key="ServiceUrl">https://api.crmcompany.com/v1/getUserData</Item>
      <Item Key="SendClaimsIn">Body</Item>
      <Item Key="AuthenticationType">Bearer</Item>
      <Item Key="BearerToken">your-secret-token</Item>
    </Metadata>
    <InputClaims>
      <InputClaim ClaimTypeReferenceId="email" />
    </InputClaims>
    <OutputClaims>
      <OutputClaim ClaimTypeReferenceId="loyaltyStatus" />
    </OutputClaims>
    <UseTechnicalProfileForSessionManagement    ReferenceId="SM-Noop"
/>
  </Protocol>
</TechnicalProfile>
```

Here, we POST the user's email and receive `loyaltyStatus` in return.

Step 3: Add the Technical Profile to the Orchestration Flow

Integrate the above profile into your orchestration steps:

```xml
<OrchestrationStep Order="3" Type="ClaimsExchange">
  <ClaimsExchanges>
    <ClaimsExchange                            Id="Invoke-CRMData"
TechnicalProfileReferenceId="REST-GetCRMData" />
  </ClaimsExchanges>
</OrchestrationStep>
```

Ensure this step occurs after collecting the email but before issuing the token.

API Response Structure

Azure AD B2C expects a well-formed response from your REST API:

```json
{
  "version": "1.0.0",
  "status": 200,
  "loyaltyStatus": "Gold"
}
```

Optional errors:

```json
{
  "version": "1.0.0",
  "status": 400,
  "userMessage": "Unable to retrieve CRM data."
}
```

If you need to pass multiple claims:

```json
{
  "version": "1.0.0",
  "status": 200,
```

```
  "loyaltyStatus": "Gold",
  "userTier": "Premium",
  "pointsBalance": "3200"
}
```

All values must be serializable to strings and match expected claims.

Security Considerations

Since sensitive data is exchanged between Azure AD B2C and your external service, security is critical:

- **HTTPS only**: Never expose unsecured endpoints.

- **Authentication**: Use bearer tokens, mTLS, or Azure Managed Identity for calling the API.

- **Rate limiting**: Protect your API from abuse with throttling rules.

- **Input validation**: Validate all input claims before using them.

- **Logging**: Log usage, errors, and security events in your API.

Never log personally identifiable information (PII) in plain text.

Use Case Examples

Subscription Access Control

A user may have purchased a premium plan outside Azure. Use an external API to validate their subscription before allowing access.

External API Returns:

```
{
  "subscriptionStatus": "Active",
  "plan": "Pro"
}
```

Terms of Service Enforcement

Check an external database for TOS acceptance.

Return:

```
{
  "tosAccepted": true,
  "acceptedDate": "2024-12-01"
}
```

Location-Based Claims

Geo-locate the user or determine their nearest region for data sovereignty.

Return:

```
{
  "region": "UK-South",
  "complianceLevel": "Tier-1"
}
```

Performance Optimization

- **Cache results**: Use short-lived caching to avoid repeated lookups.

- **Minimal response**: Only return necessary claims.

- **Compress responses**: Enable gzip if your backend supports it.

- **Batching**: Aggregate data from multiple sources in a single call where possible.

- **Timeouts**: Set timeouts on both client and server to avoid hanging flows.

Common Pitfalls

- **Missing claim definitions**: Claims returned by the API must be defined in the policy file.

- **Mismatched data types**: Avoid sending integers or booleans; B2C expects strings.

- **Unauthorized APIs**: Ensure token-based APIs are correctly validated.

- **Incorrect step order**: Ensure your API step is after collecting input but before token issuance.

- **No error response**: If the API crashes without returning JSON, B2C will fail silently or with a generic error.

Logging and Monitoring

Use **Application Insights** and **Azure Monitor** for:

- Logging   policy   execution

- Identifying   failed   external   calls

- Tracking   claim   values   over   time

- Alerting   on   failure   rates

Also monitor your external API for:

- Latency   spikes

- Rate-limit   hits

- Failed   authentications

Future Enhancements

- **GraphQL Integration**: B2C doesn't natively support GraphQL yet, but you can use a middleware   to   translate.

- **Azure Event Grid Triggers**: Trigger user data refresh asynchronously using user sign-in   events.

- **Database-level integration**: Securely expose only whitelisted identity claims through an   API   that   fronts   your   database.

Summary

Integrating external claims sources with Azure AD B2C enables dynamic, real-time customization of the identity experience. From retrieving subscription data to enforcing access rules or personalizing content, external claims turn B2C into a smart, responsive identity platform.

By defining custom claims, securely connecting to external systems, and embedding those claims into user journeys, you unlock powerful scenarios that go far beyond static configuration. With proper planning, performance tuning, and security practices, external claims can become a reliable cornerstone of your user experience strategy.

Session and Token Lifetimes Configuration

Controlling session behavior and token lifetimes in Azure AD B2C is essential for balancing security, usability, and performance in your application ecosystem. Whether you're developing a consumer-facing portal, a mobile app, or a SaaS platform, you'll need to define how long users stay signed in, how frequently they must reauthenticate, and how tokens are issued and validated. This section explores the full range of capabilities for configuring session and token lifetimes in both built-in user flows and custom policies using the Identity Experience Framework (IEF).

We will cover session settings, token validity periods, refresh token policies, Single Sign-On (SSO) configuration, and techniques for enforcing reauthentication under specific scenarios. Practical code examples and policy snippets are included throughout.

Understanding Token Types in Azure AD B2C

Azure AD B2C issues several types of tokens during authentication:

- **ID Token**: Contains claims about the user, used by the client app to understand who is signed in.

- **Access Token**: Used to authorize API calls.

- **Refresh Token**: Allows the client to get new tokens without prompting the user to sign in again.

Each of these has its own configurable lifetime. In addition, session cookies and SSO tokens dictate how often users must reauthenticate.

Configuring Token Lifetimes in Built-In User Flows

For applications using built-in policies, token lifetimes can be managed through Azure AD B2C settings, but with limited customization.

Step 1: Create a Token Lifetime Policy

Token lifetime policies are created using Microsoft Graph or PowerShell, as they're not exposed in the Azure Portal for B2C.

Example PowerShell to create a token lifetime policy:

```
Connect-AzureAD

New-AzureADPolicy                          -Definition
@('{"TokenLifetimePolicy":{"Version":1,"AccessTokenLifetime":"01:00:
00","MaxAgeSingleFactor":"00:30:00"}}') `
  -DisplayName "B2C Token Policy" `
  -IsOrganizationDefault $false `
  -Type "TokenLifetimePolicy"
```

This sets:

- Access   token   lifetime   to   1   hour
- Max   SSO   session   age   to   30   minutes   (forces   reauthentication)

Step 2: Assign the Policy to an App

```
$app = Get-AzureADApplication -Filter "DisplayName eq 'MyB2CApp'"
Add-AzureADApplicationPolicy    -Id    $app.ObjectId    -RefObjectId
<PolicyId>
```

Note: Token lifetime policies may not be fully supported in B2C tenants created after 2021 due to migration to continuous access evaluation (CAE).

Configuring Token Lifetimes in Custom Policies

In custom policies, you have granular control over lifetimes using the `TokenLifetimeSeconds`, `SessionExpiryType`, and `SessionExpiryInSeconds` metadata fields within technical profiles.

Example: Setting Token Lifetimes in a Relying Party Policy

```
<RelyingParty>
  <DefaultUserJourney ReferenceId="SignUpOrSignIn" />
  <TechnicalProfile Id="JwtIssuer">
    <DisplayName>JWT Issuer</DisplayName>
    <Protocol Name="None" />
    <OutputTokenFormat>JWT</OutputTokenFormat>
    <Metadata>
      <Item Key="token_lifetime_secs">3600</Item> <!-- 1 hour -->
      <Item Key="id_token_lifetime_secs">1800</Item> <!-- 30 mins --
>
      <Item Key="refresh_token_lifetime_secs">1209600</Item> <!-- 14
days -->
    </Metadata>
  </TechnicalProfile>
</RelyingParty>
```

Each key controls a specific aspect of the token experience:

- `token_lifetime_secs`: Access token validity

- `id_token_lifetime_secs`: ID token validity

- `refresh_token_lifetime_secs`: Refresh token expiration

This configuration is critical for determining how frequently clients must refresh tokens and how long an issued token can be trusted without reauthentication.

Controlling Session Expiry and SSO Behavior

Session management in Azure AD B2C involves cookies and backend session controls that dictate how long users remain authenticated across applications.

Example: Session Expiry Configuration

You can configure session expiration in the `SessionManagement` section of a relying party policy or directly in a technical profile.

```
<SessionManagement>
  <SessionExpiryType>Absolute</SessionExpiryType>
```

```
<SessionExpiryInSeconds>1800</SessionExpiryInSeconds>    <!--    30
minutes -->
</SessionManagement>
```

- `Absolute`: The session ends after a fixed duration, regardless of activity.

- `Rolling`: The session expiry resets with user activity (less secure but user-friendly).

For example, an absolute timeout of 30 minutes ensures users must reauthenticate after that time, even if they are active.

Single Sign-On (SSO) Between Applications

Azure AD B2C supports SSO across apps registered in the same tenant. To enable and control SSO:

1. Ensure applications share the same B2C tenant and are registered properly.

2. Use consistent session cookies and policies.

Example: Enabling SSO in a Technical Profile

```
<Metadata>
  <Item Key="SingleSignOn">true</Item>
  <Item Key="SessionExpiryType">Absolute</Item>
  <Item Key="SessionExpiryInSeconds">3600</Item>
</Metadata>
```

To disable SSO (forcing login every time):

```
<Metadata>
  <Item Key="SingleSignOn">false</Item>
</Metadata>
```

SSO tokens are managed using browser cookies. Clearing cookies or using different browsers will bypass SSO unless persistent cookies are used.

Reauthentication Scenarios

In certain cases, you may want to require users to reauthenticate:

- Accessing sensitive areas (e.g., payment info)

- Performing high-risk operations (e.g., changing password)

- After a long period of inactivity

Use orchestration steps and technical profiles to enforce this:

```
<OrchestrationStep Order="3" Type="ClaimsExchange">
  <Preconditions>
    <Precondition Type="ClaimEquals" ExecuteActionsIf="true">
      <Value>forceReauth</Value>
      <Value>true</Value>
      <Action>SkipThisOrchestrationStep</Action>
    </Precondition>
  </Preconditions>
  <ClaimsExchanges>
    <ClaimsExchange                          Id="DoInteractiveLogin"
TechnicalProfileReferenceId="SelfAsserted-LocalAccountSignin-
Username" />
  </ClaimsExchanges>
</OrchestrationStep>
```

Set the `forceReauth` claim dynamically or via REST API connector to trigger login under specific business conditions.

Refresh Token Behavior

Refresh tokens are issued if you request the `offline_access` scope. Clients use refresh tokens to get new access/ID tokens without the user signing in again.

Key Points:

- Refresh tokens are long-lived (typically 14 days, configurable).

- They can be revoked by changing credentials or user account settings.

- They support **rolling** behavior — a new refresh token is issued every time a new access token is requested.

Example: Enabling Refresh Token Flow in OAuth2

Request the scope during login:

```
openid profile offline_access
```

Token request using refresh token:

```
POST /<tenant>.onmicrosoft.com/oauth2/v2.0/token
Content-Type: application/x-www-form-urlencoded

grant_type=refresh_token
&client_id=YOUR_CLIENT_ID
&refresh_token=YOUR_REFRESH_TOKEN
&scope=openid profile
```

Make sure your app is configured to allow refresh tokens (in the Azure Portal under API permissions).

Troubleshooting Token and Session Issues

Some common issues and how to resolve them:

- **Token Expired Immediately**: Check that system clocks are synced and lifetimes are properly configured.

- **Refresh Token Not Returned**: Ensure `offline_access` scope is requested and app permissions are correctly configured.

- **SSO Not Working**: Make sure session cookies are not blocked and applications share the same domain and tenant.

- **Unexpected Logouts**: Check session expiration settings and browser cookie behavior.

Use **Application Insights** to monitor session durations and token issuance events for auditing and debugging.

Best Practices

- Use **shorter access token lifetimes** (15-60 minutes) for enhanced security.

- **Avoid long sessions** in shared or public environments.

- **Use refresh tokens** to maintain usability without reauthentication.

- **Reauthenticate** before sensitive operations.

- **Disable SSO** in high-security applications to prevent unintended access.

- **Log token issuance** and usage to monitor for anomalies.

Summary

Controlling session and token lifetimes in Azure AD B2C allows you to fine-tune user experiences and security boundaries. Whether you're building a frictionless user journey for e-commerce or enforcing strict compliance in a finance application, understanding how and when tokens are issued, refreshed, and expired is essential.

Using custom policies, you can precisely control token durations, enforce reauthentication rules, and implement robust SSO strategies. With careful configuration, you can achieve a balance between convenience and control that supports your application's security and performance requirements.

Managing Identity Transformation with Claims

In Azure AD B2C, claims are the fundamental building blocks of identity transactions. They represent user attributes (like `email`, `givenName`, `role`) and system metadata (like `authenticationSource`, `identityProvider`). Identity transformation with claims refers to the process of manipulating, evaluating, combining, or mapping these claims to enforce business logic, integrate with third-party systems, and control what is ultimately passed to applications and tokens.

This section provides an in-depth exploration of how to manage identity transformation using claims within custom policies. You'll learn how to create and extend claims, perform conditional logic, concatenate or transform values, and use claims to drive user journeys. Examples are provided in XML, with full explanations of the Identity Experience Framework (IEF) structures involved.

Types of Claim Transformations

Claim transformations can take many forms:

- **Mapping**: Changing the name or format of an incoming claim.

- **Concatenation**: Combining multiple claims into one.

- **Conditional Evaluation**: Determining values based on other claim values.

- **Value Injection**: Inserting hardcoded or system-generated values.

- **Normalization**: Formatting claims (e.g., trimming, lowercasing).

- **Derived Claims**: Calculating one claim based on the value of others.

Azure AD B2C supports these via the `ClaimsTransformation` element in XML policies, which can be invoked in technical profiles.

Creating a Simple Claims Transformation

A `ClaimsTransformation` uses a `TransformationMethod`, which defines what operation to perform. Let's create a transformation that uppercases the domain part of an email address.

Step 1: Define Input and Output Claims

```
<ClaimType Id="domainUppercase">
  <DisplayName>Domain Uppercase</DisplayName>
  <DataType>string</DataType>
</ClaimType>
```

Step 2: Create the Claims Transformation

```
<ClaimsTransformation                              Id="UppercaseDomain"
TransformationMethod="FormatStringClaim">
  <InputClaims>
    <InputClaim                           ClaimTypeReferenceId="email"
TransformationClaimType="inputClaim" />
  </InputClaims>
  <InputParameters>
    <InputParameter Id="stringFormat">user@{0:U}</InputParameter>
```

```
    </InputParameters>
    <OutputClaims>
      <OutputClaim                ClaimTypeReferenceId="domainUppercase"
TransformationClaimType="outputClaim" />
    </OutputClaims>
</ClaimsTransformation>
```

This transformation uppercases the domain using string formatting. $\{0:U\}$ indicates an uppercase transformation.

Common Transformation Methods

Azure AD B2C supports a variety of transformation methods, including:

- `FormatStringClaim`
- `AssertBooleanClaimIsEqualToValue`
- `CopyClaim`
- `CreateStringClaim`
- `RegexMatch`
- `DateTimeComparison`
- `StringComparison`
- `StringConcatenation`
- `RegexReplace`
- `GetClaimFromAlternativeSecurityId`
- `LookupValue`

Each method requires specific parameters and is suited to a different use case.

Real-World Example: Assigning User Roles

Imagine your user database does not store roles directly but uses a value like `accountType` with values `admin`, `standard`, `viewer`. You want to translate this into a `role` claim used by your applications.

Step 1: Define the Role Claim

```xml
<ClaimType Id="role">
  <DisplayName>User Role</DisplayName>
  <DataType>string</DataType>
  <DefaultPartnerClaimTypes>
    <Protocol Name="OAuth2" PartnerClaimType="role" />
  </DefaultPartnerClaimTypes>
</ClaimType>
```

Step 2: Create Transformation for Role Mapping

```xml
<ClaimsTransformation                         Id="MapAccountTypeToRole"
TransformationMethod="FormatStringClaim">
  <InputClaims>
    <InputClaim                 ClaimTypeReferenceId="accountType"
TransformationClaimType="inputClaim" />
  </InputClaims>
  <InputParameters>
    <InputParameter Id="stringFormat">{0}</InputParameter>
  </InputParameters>
  <OutputClaims>
    <OutputClaim                      ClaimTypeReferenceId="role"
TransformationClaimType="outputClaim" />
  </OutputClaims>
</ClaimsTransformation>
```

You could also use conditional logic:

```xml
<ClaimsTransformation                            Id="AssignAdminRole"
TransformationMethod="AssertBooleanClaimIsEqualToValue">
  <InputClaims>
    <InputClaim                  ClaimTypeReferenceId="accountType"
TransformationClaimType="inputClaim" />
  </InputClaims>
  <InputParameters>
```

```
    <InputParameter Id="valueToCompareTo">admin</InputParameter>
  </InputParameters>
  <OutputClaims>
    <OutputClaim                        ClaimTypeReferenceId="role"
TransformationClaimType="outputClaim" />
  </OutputClaims>
</ClaimsTransformation>
```

Chaining Multiple Transformations

You can chain claims transformations by executing them in sequence within a technical profile.
This is useful when you need to manipulate multiple claims or perform layered logic.

Example: Normalize Username

- Lowercase   the   username

- Trim   whitespace

- Prefix   with   usr_


```
<ClaimsTransformation                               Id="TrimUsername"
TransformationMethod="StringTrim">
  <InputClaims>
    <InputClaim                       ClaimTypeReferenceId="username"
TransformationClaimType="inputClaim" />
  </InputClaims>
  <OutputClaims>
    <OutputClaim              ClaimTypeReferenceId="usernameTrimmed"
TransformationClaimType="outputClaim" />
  </OutputClaims>
</ClaimsTransformation>

<ClaimsTransformation                          Id="LowercaseUsername"
TransformationMethod="StringCaseConversion">
  <InputClaims>
    <InputClaim               ClaimTypeReferenceId="usernameTrimmed"
TransformationClaimType="inputClaim" />
  </InputClaims>
  <InputParameters>
```

```
    <InputParameter Id="case">lower</InputParameter>
  </InputParameters>
  <OutputClaims>
    <OutputClaim                    ClaimTypeReferenceId="usernameLower"
TransformationClaimType="outputClaim" />
  </OutputClaims>
</ClaimsTransformation>

<ClaimsTransformation                              Id="PrefixUsername"
TransformationMethod="FormatStringClaim">
  <InputClaims>
    <InputClaim                     ClaimTypeReferenceId="usernameLower"
TransformationClaimType="inputClaim" />
  </InputClaims>
  <InputParameters>
    <InputParameter Id="stringFormat">usr_{0}</InputParameter>
  </InputParameters>
  <OutputClaims>
    <OutputClaim              ClaimTypeReferenceId="usernameFormatted"
TransformationClaimType="outputClaim" />
  </OutputClaims>
</ClaimsTransformation>
```

Each transformation prepares the claim for the next step, ultimately resulting in a fully formatted username.

Using Conditional Logic

To alter the flow based on claim values, you can use Preconditions or create conditional ClaimsTransformations.

Example: Skipping MFA for Trusted Users

```
<Precondition Type="ClaimEquals" ExecuteActionsIf="true">
  <Value>userTrustLevel</Value>
  <Value>high</Value>
  <Action>SkipThisOrchestrationStep</Action>
</Precondition>
```

In this case, a user with userTrustLevel equal to high will skip MFA.

Regular Expressions for Claim Manipulation

Regex-based transformations are powerful for extracting or reformatting claims.

Example: Extract Domain from Email

```
<ClaimsTransformation                           Id="ExtractEmailDomain"
TransformationMethod="RegexMatch">
  <InputClaims>
    <InputClaim                          ClaimTypeReferenceId="email"
TransformationClaimType="inputClaim" />
  </InputClaims>
  <InputParameters>
    <InputParameter Id="pattern">@(.+)</InputParameter>
    <InputParameter Id="group">1</InputParameter>
  </InputParameters>
  <OutputClaims>
    <OutputClaim                   ClaimTypeReferenceId="emailDomain"
TransformationClaimType="outputClaim" />
  </OutputClaims>
</ClaimsTransformation>
```

This captures the domain part of the email using regex and stores it in emailDomain.

Enforcing Business Logic with Lookup Tables

Azure AD B2C allows static value mapping via the LookupValue transformation method.

Example: Map Country Code to Region

```
<ClaimsTransformation                          Id="MapCountryToRegion"
TransformationMethod="LookupValue">
  <InputClaims>
    <InputClaim                          ClaimTypeReferenceId="country"
TransformationClaimType="inputClaim" />
  </InputClaims>
  <InputParameters>
    <InputParameter Id="valueMap">
      US=NorthAmerica
```

```
        DE=Europe
        JP=Asia
      </InputParameter>
    </InputParameters>
    <OutputClaims>
      <OutputClaim                        ClaimTypeReferenceId="userRegion"
TransformationClaimType="outputClaim" />
    </OutputClaims>
</ClaimsTransformation>
```

This can simplify region-specific logic across your policies.

Output Claims to Applications

Finally, any transformed claims you wish to pass to applications must be:

1. Defined   in   `ClaimType`   with   proper   `PartnerClaimType`   mapping.

2. Included   in   the   `OutputClaims`   of   the   final   `JwtIssuer`   technical   profile.

Example:

```
<TechnicalProfile Id="JwtIssuer">
  <OutputClaims>
    <OutputClaim                    ClaimTypeReferenceId="usernameFormatted"
PartnerClaimType="username" />
    <OutputClaim ClaimTypeReferenceId="role" PartnerClaimType="role"
/>
    <OutputClaim                        ClaimTypeReferenceId="userRegion"
PartnerClaimType="region" />
  </OutputClaims>
</TechnicalProfile>
```

Best Practices

*   Define   reusable   `ClaimTypes`   for   all   transformed   claims.

- Use descriptive IDs for transformations (`PrefixUsername`, `AssignAdminRole`, etc.).

- Chain transformations logically and modularly.

- Avoid hardcoding values directly in policies unless static.

- Always test transformations using Application Insights or verbose logging.

Summary

Claims transformation in Azure AD B2C is a powerful mechanism for shaping the identity lifecycle to meet your application's needs. Whether mapping user types, normalizing input, extracting values, or enforcing dynamic logic, you can leverage IEF's `ClaimsTransformation` infrastructure to build adaptable, secure, and context-aware user journeys.

By mastering this capability, you enable fine-grained control over identity flows that support both scalability and sophistication—key ingredients for modern identity-driven applications.

Chapter 8: Testing, Debugging, and Logging

Local Debugging Techniques

Debugging and testing Azure AD B2C implementations locally is an essential part of a robust identity solution deployment process. Before pushing your configuration to production environments, it's important to validate user flows, custom policies, and application integrations to ensure the system behaves as expected and that users experience seamless journeys.

This section provides deep insights into how you can effectively debug Azure AD B2C setups locally, including custom policies, claims transformations, REST API connectors, and token acquisition. We'll also explore helpful strategies for isolating errors and improving turnaround time during development.

Understanding the Debugging Context

Azure AD B2C is a cloud-hosted service, and because of that, most of the debugging must occur through cloud-executed policies. However, there are many components that can and should be tested and debugged locally before deployment to Azure:

- XML files for custom policies (trust frameworks)
- JavaScript and HTML for customized UI
- REST API endpoints called within the user flow
- Token acquisition flows in SPAs or mobile apps
- Token decoding and validation in backend APIs

Debugging Custom Policies

Custom policies are written using XML and follow a schema defined by the Identity Experience Framework (IEF). These policies can be intricate, consisting of multiple elements such as OrchestrationSteps, ClaimsTransformations, and TechnicalProfiles.

Best Practices for Debugging Custom Policies:

1. **Schema Validation:** Use an XML linter to validate the schema of your policy files locally. IDEs like VS Code with XML extensions or JetBrains Rider can highlight

schema mismatches and misused attributes.

2. **Isolate and Test in Layers:** When building new policies, start with minimal files (Base, Extensions, RelyingParty) and test each new feature incrementally. For example, test the sign-up flow before adding REST API connectors.

Use Claim Debugging Output: Inject a debugging step to output claim values before the token issuance. Add this block to your custom policy's `RelyingParty` section:

xml

```
<OrchestrationStep Order="9" Type="ClaimsExchange">
  <ClaimsExchanges>
    <ClaimsExchange                                      Id="DebugOutput"
TechnicalProfileReferenceId="Debug-DisplayClaims" />
  </ClaimsExchanges>
</OrchestrationStep>
```

Then define the `Debug-DisplayClaims` technical profile:

xml

```
<TechnicalProfile Id="Debug-DisplayClaims">
  <DisplayName>Debug Output</DisplayName>
  <Protocol Name="Proprietary" />
  <Metadata>
    <Item Key="ContentDefinitionReferenceId">api.selfasserted</Item>
  </Metadata>
  <InputClaims>
    <InputClaim ClaimTypeReferenceId="email" />
    <InputClaim ClaimTypeReferenceId="displayName" />
    <!-- Add any claims you want to inspect -->
  </InputClaims>
  <UseTechnicalProfileForSessionManagement ReferenceId="SM-Noop" />
</TechnicalProfile>
```

3. This outputs claim values to the user, helping you see what values are being passed between steps.

4. **Debug Claims Transformation:** Use test input values and inspect outputs in your XML logic. For complex logic, you may replicate transformation behavior in a local script using Python or Node.js to validate the logic.

REST API Debugging

RESTful API connectors are a common point of failure in Azure AD B2C flows. They are invoked mid-journey to enrich claims or call external systems. Misconfigurations often lead to 500 errors or blocked flows.

Steps for Local Testing:

- **Postman Testing:** Before deploying the REST endpoint into your policy, test it using Postman or curl. Ensure your API:

    o Responds within 2 seconds (default timeout)

    o Returns a 200 status with a JSON payload in the correct format

    o Handles missing or incorrect claims gracefully

Mock Locally with Express or FastAPI: Use a lightweight local server to simulate the REST API if the actual service is not ready. Example with Node.js/Express:

javascript

```javascript
const express = require('express');
const app = express();
app.use(express.json());

app.post('/api/enrich', (req, res) => {
  const input = req.body;
  res.json({
    isPremiumUser: true,
    loyaltyPoints: 1200,
  });
});

app.listen(3000, () => console.log('Mock API running on port 3000'));
```

-
- **Enable Logging in Your API:** Ensure detailed logging of requests and responses in your service to troubleshoot unexpected behavior during policy execution.

Debugging Single-Page Applications (SPA)

When integrating with SPAs like React or Angular, it's important to verify token acquisition and user flow redirection. The MSAL (Microsoft Authentication Library) enables this integration.

Debugging Tips:

- **Use Browser Dev Tools:** Inspect network traffic during login redirects. Look for:

    ○ Authorization URL construction (correct tenant, policy, client ID)

    ○ Redirect URI and error messages in query params

    ○ Access and ID token issuance

Verbose Logging in MSAL:

typescript

```typescript
const msalInstance = new PublicClientApplication({
  auth: {
    clientId: 'YOUR_CLIENT_ID',
    authority:
'https://<tenant>.b2clogin.com/tfp/<tenant>.onmicrosoft.com/B2C_1_si
gnupsignin1',
    redirectUri: '/',
  },
  system: {
    loggerOptions: {
      loggerCallback: (level, message) => {
        console.log(message);
      },
      logLevel: LogLevel.Verbose,
    },
  },
});
```

- This provides insight into token caching, authority resolution, and error details.

- **Handle MSAL Errors:** Use try/catch blocks around login methods and handle known error codes like `interaction_required`, `login_required`, etc.

Backend API Debugging

When your backend API validates B2C-issued tokens, problems often arise from:

- Misconfigured `issuer` or `audience` in validation
- Incorrect token scopes
- Clock drift issues

Token Validation Tips:

1. **Decode Tokens Locally:** Use jwt.ms or `jwt.io` to paste and inspect tokens. This helps verify:

   - Claim values
   - Expiration time
   - Audience (aud)
   - Issuer (iss)

Local Validation Code (Node.js with jsonwebtoken):

javascript

```javascript
const jwt = require('jsonwebtoken');
const fs = require('fs');
const token = 'ey...'; // JWT token from frontend

const publicKey = fs.readFileSync('public.pem'); // Get from B2C
OpenID config

jwt.verify(token, publicKey, { algorithms: ['RS256'], audience:
'YOUR_API_ID' }, (err, decoded) => {
  if (err) {
    console.error('Invalid token:', err);
  } else {
    console.log('Valid token:', decoded);
  }
});
```

2.

Configure   Middleware   Correctly: In   ASP.NET   Core,   for   example:

csharp

```
services.AddAuthentication(JwtBearerDefaults.AuthenticationScheme)
    .AddJwtBearer(options =>
    {
        options.Authority                                           =
"https://<tenant>.b2clogin.com/<tenant>.onmicrosoft.com/B2C_1_signup
signin1/v2.0/";
        options.Audience = "<your-api-client-id>";
    });
```

3.

Workflow for Iterative Debugging

Debugging B2C integrations can be cyclical. Use this workflow for consistent success:

1. **Start with UI and Flow Tests:** Run the user flow directly from Azure Portal and confirm basic functionality.

2. **Validate Tokens:** Acquire tokens using your app or Postman and inspect them manually.

3. **Test REST APIs Separately:** Ensure your external APIs work independently before wiring them into a policy.

4. **Use Logs:** Enable App Insights (covered in 8.2) to trace execution steps.

5. **Rollback Approach:** Always version your XML files. If new changes break flows, revert to the last known working version.

Common Issues and Fixes

Symptom	Cause	Fix
Blank screen after redirect	JavaScript error or redirect loop	Check console logs, MSAL config

"AADB2C90077" error	REST API did not respond correctly	Check response format, latency
Token missing custom claims	Incorrect claims transformation or step order	Inspect orchestration steps
"invalid_client" error	Wrong client ID or secret	Verify Azure Portal values
Token validation fails	Wrong audience or missing public keys	Match aud, ensure proper JWKs

Conclusion

Local debugging of Azure AD B2C configurations is a meticulous but essential task that ensures the stability and correctness of your identity management system. From policy validation and UI tweaks to token handling and REST API integration, every component benefits from a structured and layered approach to testing. By mastering these debugging techniques, developers can deploy with confidence, knowing their identity flows will operate securely and reliably under real-world conditions.

Using Application Insights

Azure Application Insights is a powerful monitoring and diagnostics tool that provides deep insights into the behavior and performance of applications, including those integrated with Azure Active Directory B2C. While most commonly used with web applications and APIs, Application Insights can be a critical tool in the toolkit of anyone working with custom policies, user journeys, and backend integrations within Azure AD B2C.

This section explores how to enable and leverage Application Insights within Azure AD B2C to trace user journeys, capture policy errors, monitor REST API calls, and gain visibility into identity experience performance. By the end of this section, you'll be able to use Application Insights as a real-time debugging and analytics platform for your identity system.

Enabling Application Insights in Azure AD B2C

Application Insights can be integrated with Azure AD B2C by associating an Application Insights resource with your B2C tenant. This enables detailed logging for built-in and custom policies.

Steps to Enable Application Insights:

1. **Create an Application Insights Resource:**
   - Go to the Azure Portal.
   - Search for "Application Insights" and click "Create."
   - Select your subscription, resource group, region, and give it a name.
   - Choose "General" for Application Type.

2. **Connect Application Insights to Your B2C Tenant:**
   - Navigate to your Azure AD B2C tenant in the Azure portal.
   - Select **User Flows** or **Identity Experience Framework** depending on your setup.
   - Click on **Audit Logs** or select a specific policy to modify.
   - Under **Application Insights**, paste your Instrumentation Key.

Alternatively, add this key in the **TrustFrameworkExtensions.xml** custom policy file:

xml

```
<Diagnostics>
  <InstrumentationKey>Your-Instrumentation-Key</InstrumentationKey>
</Diagnostics>
```

3. This block should be placed inside the `<TrustFrameworkPolicy>` element, directly under the `<BasePolicy>` node.

How Logging Works with Custom Policies

Once configured, Application Insights starts collecting telemetry from executed policies. The diagnostic information includes:

- Timestamped logs of each orchestration step.
- Input and output claims at each step.
- TechnicalProfile execution details.

- REST   API   call   payloads   and   results.

- Errors,   warnings,   and   trace   messages.

This data becomes invaluable for understanding the behavior of your policies and identifying exactly where and why a flow may be failing.

Example Output Snippet from Application Insights:

```json
{
  "step": "OrchestrationStep5",
  "technicalProfile": "REST-GetUserInfo",
  "claims": {
    "email": "test@example.com",
    "isLoyaltyUser": "true"
  },
  "status": "Succeeded",
  "timestamp": "2025-04-02T14:20:01.123Z"
}
```

Querying Logs in Application Insights

Application Insights supports a powerful query language called Kusto Query Language (KQL). This lets you run detailed queries against your logs to find patterns, anomalies, and specific events.

Basic Query to See All Log Entries:

```
traces
| where timestamp > ago(1d)
| where customDimensions.PolicyName == "B2C_1A_signup"
| project timestamp, message, customDimensions.OrchestrationStep,
customDimensions.TechnicalProfile
```

Filter by Failed REST Calls:

```
traces
| where customDimensions.TechnicalProfile contains "REST"
| where message contains "Error"
```

```
| project timestamp, message, customDimensions.RequestBody,
customDimensions.Response
```

Search for Specific User ID:

```
traces
| where customDimensions.UserId == "abc12345"
| project timestamp, message
```

These queries can be saved and reused to continuously monitor specific policies or to automate alerting and diagnostics.

Interpreting Logs and Diagnosing Failures

Application Insights makes it much easier to find the root cause of issues in your B2C flows. Here are some common log types and how to interpret them:

1. OrchestrationStep Failures:

When a specific step fails, look for entries where `status != Succeeded`. Check:

- Which step failed
- Which TechnicalProfile was invoked
- What input claims were passed
- Whether the output claims are empty or malformed

2. REST API Call Failures:

If your logs contain `REST-` prefixes, those typically indicate API calls within your policy. Review:

- Request headers/body (e.g., malformed JSON)
- Timeout issues (default timeout is 2 seconds)
- Unauthorized access or wrong endpoints

3. User Input Errors:

Sometimes users enter incorrect data that causes a flow to fail. Application Insights will capture claim values entered before the failure and can help you recreate the scenario.

4. Unexpected Token Format:

If your final `issueToken` step fails, inspect the `RelyingParty` technical profile logs. Check for missing or invalid claims needed in the token.

Enhancing Policies with Custom Logging

You can augment the logs further by embedding custom trace messages in your custom policies using the `RaiseError` or `DisplayControl` profiles.

Example: Inject a Custom Trace Log Step

Add a dummy step that logs internal values:

```
<TechnicalProfile Id="LogCustomTrace">
  <DisplayName>Log Trace</DisplayName>
  <Protocol Name="Proprietary" />
  <Metadata>
    <Item Key="IncludeInTelemetry">true</Item>
  </Metadata>
  <InputClaims>
    <InputClaim ClaimTypeReferenceId="userType" />
    <InputClaim ClaimTypeReferenceId="locale" />
  </InputClaims>
</TechnicalProfile>
```

Then call it in your orchestration steps:

```
<OrchestrationStep Order="3" Type="ClaimsExchange">
  <ClaimsExchanges>
    <ClaimsExchange                          Id="LogTrace"
TechnicalProfileReferenceId="LogCustomTrace" />
  </ClaimsExchanges>
</OrchestrationStep>
```

This will inject claims into your telemetry stream for analysis.

Correlating with Frontend and Backend Logs

Application Insights provides an end-to-end view, but it becomes even more powerful when correlated with logs from your frontend (SPA/mobile app) and backend APIs.

Frontend Integration:

Use the Application Insights JavaScript SDK in your frontend to log client-side metrics:

```
import { ApplicationInsights } from '@microsoft/applicationinsights-web';

const appInsights = new ApplicationInsights({
  config: {
    instrumentationKey: 'your-key-here',
    enableAutoRouteTracking: true
  }
});
appInsights.loadAppInsights();
appInsights.trackPageView();
```

You can then use the same User ID or Session ID to correlate logs from your custom policies with frontend events.

Backend Correlation:

In APIs protected by Azure AD B2C-issued tokens, extract the `sub` or `oid` claim from tokens and log them into App Insights or your backend telemetry store. This creates a full trail of user interactions across layers.

Setting Up Alerts and Dashboards

Once your B2C flows emit telemetry, use Application Insights features like Alerts and Workbooks to automate monitoring.

Setting Up Alerts:

- Go to Application Insights > Alerts.

- Create a new condition based on a KQL query (e.g., failed REST calls > 5 in 10 mins).

- Set an action group (email, webhook, etc.) to notify your team.

Creating Dashboards:

Build visual dashboards to summarize:

- Number of sign-ups and sign-ins

- Failed authentication attempts

- REST API latency and error rates

- User journey completion rates

This gives stakeholders visibility without needing to dive into raw telemetry.

Limitations and Considerations

While Application Insights is extremely useful, be aware of these points:

- **Latency:** Logs are near-real-time but may take a few seconds to appear.

- **Retention:** Logs are retained for 90 days by default, extendable via Azure Monitor.

- **Security:** Don't log sensitive data such as passwords or personal identifiers.

- **Cost:** High-volume logging can become expensive. Sample data or log selectively.

Conclusion

Application Insights transforms Azure AD B2C from a black-box identity engine into a transparent, traceable system that developers and administrators can monitor, debug, and optimize. With detailed orchestration logs, REST API telemetry, KQL querying, and integration with frontend/backend systems, it empowers you to deliver a secure, performant, and user-friendly authentication experience. Whether you are troubleshooting a broken policy or analyzing trends in user behavior, Application Insights is your essential tool for deep visibility into your identity platform.

Diagnosing Common Errors

When implementing Azure AD B2C, diagnosing errors is one of the most important aspects of ensuring a smooth identity experience for users. Azure AD B2C leverages a wide range of components, including user flows, custom policies, REST API connectors, identity providers, and application integrations. Each of these components can introduce their own set of challenges. Understanding the structure and semantics of common error codes and scenarios can significantly reduce time spent troubleshooting and improve solution stability.

This section explores how to diagnose, interpret, and resolve the most common errors encountered in Azure AD B2C deployments, particularly when working with custom policies and integrations. You'll learn how to use logs, error messages, and platform tools to your advantage, and how to implement proactive patterns to prevent common issues from surfacing.

Understanding B2C Error Surfaces

Errors in Azure AD B2C can surface in various places:

- **Portal User Flows**: Failures show up as portal-level errors or generic messages to the end user.

- **Custom Policies**: Failures often result in cryptic error codes, stack traces, or HTTP 500 errors.

- **Application Logs**: Application Insights, browser console, or API logs reveal additional context.

- **Client Applications**: Errors appear during token acquisition, sign-in, or token validation.

Diagnosing issues effectively requires gathering error details from all relevant touchpoints.

Categorizing B2C Errors

To effectively address issues, it helps to categorize them:

Category	Description	Examples
Policy Errors	Errors in XML structure or execution logic	Orchestration failures, invalid claims
Integration Errors	Misconfigurations between B2C and external systems	REST API call failures, token misalignment
User Errors	Caused by invalid input or behavior	Invalid email, password too short

Platform Errors	Azure infrastructure issues	Internal service errors, throttling

Common Error Messages and How to Handle Them

Below is a list of frequently encountered error messages and guidance on diagnosing and resolving each.

Error: `AADB2C90077: The resource owner password credentials grant does not work with federated IdPs.`

Cause: Attempting to use ROPC (Resource Owner Password Credentials) flow with a federated identity provider (e.g., Google, Facebook).

Solution: ROPC is only supported for local accounts. Do not use it with federated IdPs.

Fix: Ensure that ROPC policies (like `B2C_1A_ROPC_Auth`) are only configured to use local accounts.

```
<TechnicalProfile Id="SelfAsserted-LocalAccountSignin-Email">
  <DisplayName>Local Account Signin</DisplayName>
  <Protocol Name="Proprietary" />
  ...
</TechnicalProfile>
```

Error: `AADB2C90091: The user has cancelled entering self-asserted information.`

Cause: The user clicked "Cancel" during a self-asserted step (e.g., sign-up form).

Solution: This is a non-critical error. Handle it gracefully in your client application and allow the user to restart the journey if needed.

Error: `AADB2C90046: The underlying REST API returned an error. Correlation ID: <guid>.`

Cause: Your RESTful API connector responded with an HTTP status code >= 400.

Solution: Review Application Insights logs using the Correlation ID. Check the API response and validate the required headers, status code, and response schema.

Fix: Ensure your API returns a valid 200 response with a correct JSON body. Example:

```
{
  "isLoyaltyUser": true,
  "loyaltyPoints": 1500
}
```

Also, return `application/json` as the Content-Type and respond within 2 seconds to avoid timeouts.

Error: `AADB2C90037: Policy '<policy-name>' does not exist.`

Cause: You're attempting to invoke a policy that hasn't been uploaded or is misspelled.

Solution:

- Check that the policy exists under **Identity Experience Framework > Custom Policies** in the portal.

- Confirm the policy name in the application configuration (e.g., in MSAL or the appsettings.json) matches exactly.

Error: `AADB2C: An exception has occurred. Correlation ID: <guid>.`

Cause: A generic error occurred in your policy execution.

Solution: Use the Correlation ID to search in Application Insights. Filter logs by:

```
traces
| where customDimensions.CorrelationId == "<guid>"
```

Check the last orchestration step and the associated TechnicalProfile for missing claims, invalid metadata, or transformation logic.

Error: `IDX10501: Signature validation failed. Unable to match keys.`

Cause: Your backend is validating a token using an outdated or incorrect signing key.

Solution:

- Refresh the OpenID configuration cache in your API.

- Ensure you're using the correct `issuer` and `audience` values.

- Retrieve signing keys from:

  ```
  https://<tenant>.b2clogin.com/<tenant>.onmicrosoft.com/discove
  ry/v2.0/keys?p=<policy-name>
  ```

Debugging TechnicalProfile Failures

TechnicalProfiles are often the root of policy failures. Use these techniques to narrow down issues:

1. Add Step-by-Step Output: Create intermediate TechnicalProfiles to output claim values. Temporarily replace `SelfAsserted` or `REST` steps with these profiles to isolate input/output.

2. Use Content Definitions: Customize error pages using `ContentDefinition` references that show meaningful messages.

```
<ContentDefinition Id="api.error">
  <LoadUri>https://yourcustomdomain.com/error.html</LoadUri>
</ContentDefinition>
```

3. Validate Transformation Chains: Ensure all `InputClaims` for `ClaimsTransformation`s are populated by upstream steps.

REST API Connector Troubleshooting

REST API connectors frequently introduce issues. To diagnose:

- Use `Postman` to test endpoints with expected request payloads.

- Ensure APIs require no authentication (unless configured in policy).

- Enable CORS if the API is accessed from a browser during development.

- Include detailed logging on the server side to capture inbound claims and headers.

Test Connector Locally:

```
curl -X POST https://api.example.com/validate
  -H "Content-Type: application/json"
  -d '{"email": "user@example.com", "postalCode": "90210"}'
```

Client-Side Token Acquisition Errors

Many B2C errors appear during frontend authentication using MSAL or similar libraries.

Error: `interaction_required`

Cause: Silent token acquisition failed because user interaction is needed.

Solution: Prompt the user to reauthenticate using `loginPopup()` or `loginRedirect()`.

```
msalInstance.acquireTokenSilent(...)
  .catch(error => {
    if (error instanceof InteractionRequiredAuthError) {
      return msalInstance.acquireTokenPopup(request);
    }
  });
```

Error: `invalid_client`

Cause: The client ID or secret is incorrect or missing.

Solution:

- Check your Azure portal application registration.
- Ensure the client ID and redirect URIs are properly configured.
- If using a client secret, validate it hasn't expired.

Handling Unknown Errors Gracefully

Sometimes Azure AD B2C emits generic errors that do not explain much. You can create a fallback error message strategy.

Example: Add a Final Step in Your RelyingParty Policy

```
<OrchestrationStep Order="99" Type="InvokeSubJourney">
  <Preconditions>
    <Precondition Type="ClaimEquals" ExecuteActionsIf="true">
      <Value>authenticationSource</Value>
      <Value>error</Value>
      <Action>SkipThisOrchestrationStep</Action>
    </Precondition>
  </Preconditions>
  <JourneyList>
    <Candidate SubJourneyReferenceId="ShowErrorPage" />
  </JourneyList>
</OrchestrationStep>
```

This ensures that if all else fails, users are directed to a branded error page that doesn't expose technical details.

Preventing Common Errors

Many issues can be prevented with a few proactive practices:

1. **Version Control Your Policies:** Keep all XML files under version control. Use clear commit messages and semantic versioning.

2. **Lint Your XML:** Use an XML validator to catch typos and structural issues early.

3. **Test Incrementally:** Don't introduce too many changes at once. Test each step individually.

4. **Use Environment Configurations:** Keep Dev, Test, and Prod configurations in separate policy files.

5. **Automate Tests:** Write scripts to simulate user journeys using tools like Selenium, Playwright, or Postman.

Conclusion

Diagnosing errors in Azure AD B2C requires a systematic approach, combining log analysis, policy inspection, API validation, and client debugging. While the platform can sometimes feel opaque, tools like Application Insights, Kusto queries, and custom logging make it possible to trace nearly every failure to its source. With enough practice, patterns emerge, and what once seemed like obscure error codes become recognizable signs pointing to straightforward fixes. By applying the techniques in this section, you can build a resilient and predictable identity system that stands up to real-world demands.

Security Testing and Recommendations

Security is a foundational pillar of any identity solution, and with Azure AD B2C serving as the authentication gateway for your applications, it becomes essential to rigorously test and harden your configuration. Azure AD B2C supports strong security defaults and offers customization capabilities, but these must be configured carefully to avoid vulnerabilities that may expose sensitive data or compromise user accounts.

This section provides comprehensive guidance on security testing approaches specific to Azure AD B2C implementations, as well as actionable recommendations to build a secure and resilient identity layer. Topics include penetration testing, token handling, policy protection, REST API security, and common misconfigurations.

Security Testing Principles

Security testing in the context of Azure AD B2C revolves around verifying that the identity system:

- Correctly authenticates and authorizes users
- Protects data at rest and in transit
- Prevents unauthorized access or privilege escalation
- Safeguards tokens and secrets
- Enforces strong policy and session controls

To effectively test these, your approach should combine automated scanning tools, manual assessments, and routine policy reviews.

Token Security and Testing

Tokens are the currency of identity in Azure AD B2C. Improper token handling or validation can lead to serious breaches.

Types of Tokens:

- **ID Token**: Contains user identity claims; consumed by clients.

- **Access Token**: Grants access to APIs; must be validated by the API.

- **Refresh Token**: Allows new tokens to be issued; must be securely stored.

Testing Access Token Handling:

1. **Decode the Token:** Use tools like jwt.io to inspect claims, signature algorithm, expiration, audience, and issuer.

2. **Validate Token Parameters:** Ensure the `aud` claim matches your API, `exp` is enforced, and `alg` is set to `RS256`.

3. **Attempt Replay Attacks:** Reuse old tokens to verify that your API rejects expired or invalidated tokens.

4. **Test for Improper Audience Acceptance:** Modify the `aud` claim in a token and see if your backend still accepts it (it shouldn't).

Sample Token Validation (Node.js):

```
const jwt = require('jsonwebtoken');
const jwksClient = require('jwks-rsa');

const client = jwksClient({
  jwksUri:
'https://<tenant>.b2clogin.com/<tenant>.onmicrosoft.com/discovery/v2
.0/keys?p=B2C_1A_signup'
});

function getKey(header, callback) {
  client.getSigningKey(header.kid, function(err, key) {
    const signingKey = key.getPublicKey();
    callback(null, signingKey);
  });
}

jwt.verify(token, getKey, {
  audience: 'your-api-client-id',
```

```
  issuer:
'https://<tenant>.b2clogin.com/<tenant>.onmicrosoft.com/v2.0/',
  algorithms: ['RS256']
}, function(err, decoded) {
  if (err) console.error("Token validation failed:", err);
  else console.log("Valid token:", decoded);
});
```

Custom Policy Security Hardening

Custom policies offer flexibility, but also open the door to misconfigurations.

Best Practices for Policy Files:

1. **Do Not Expose Sensitive Claims:** Never emit personally identifiable information (PII) or security-sensitive claims unless absolutely required.

Use OutputClaim Restrictions: Explicitly define `OutputClaim`s to avoid leaking all available claims.

xml

```
<OutputClaim ClaimTypeReferenceId="email" />
```

2.
3. **Avoid Overusing JavaScript:** Don't embed business logic or validation in JavaScript that can be tampered with in the browser.

4. **Restrict Redirect URIs:** Only allow trusted redirect URIs in your application registration to avoid open redirect vulnerabilities.

5. **Enforce HTTPS Everywhere:** Ensure that all endpoints and redirect URIs enforce HTTPS.

6. **Use** `UseTechnicalProfileForSessionManagement`: Always control how session tokens are managed and limit their duration and scope.

REST API Connector Security

REST APIs connected to your policies can become the weakest link if not secured properly.

Testing Your REST Endpoints:

- **Send Malformed Requests:** Test with invalid JSON, missing claims, or wrong content types to verify input validation.

- **Inject SQL or Script:** Attempt SQL injection or script injection if your endpoint processes user input.

- **Simulate Replay Attacks:** Reuse old requests and check if your endpoint reprocesses them.

- **Rate Limit Testing:** Send rapid or concurrent requests and observe if rate limiting or throttling is in place.

Secure Your REST API:

- Validate JWTs if they are required.

- Only accept the required claims.

- Return minimal data and only what's needed.

- Use `Content-Security-Policy` and other headers.

- Log suspicious activity and respond with 403/429 where appropriate.

Frontend and SPA Security

When integrating B2C into frontend apps, security hygiene is just as important.

Best Practices:

1. **Never Store Tokens in LocalStorage:** Use memory or secure cookies with appropriate flags (`HttpOnly`, `Secure`).

2. **Prevent Open Redirects:** Validate the post-login redirection endpoints.

Use MSAL Securely: Enable recommended security settings in your MSAL configuration.

typescript

```
const msalInstance = new PublicClientApplication({
  auth: {
```

```
    clientId: 'YOUR_CLIENT_ID',
    authority:
'https://<tenant>.b2clogin.com/tfp/<tenant>.onmicrosoft.com/B2C_1A_s
ignup',
    redirectUri: '/',
  },
  cache: {
    cacheLocation: 'sessionStorage',
    storeAuthStateInCookie: false,
  },
});
```

3.
4. **Enable CSP and XSS Protections:** Apply appropriate CSP rules and sanitizers to prevent script injections.

Multi-Factor Authentication (MFA) Testing

MFA is one of the most effective ways to secure identities. Azure AD B2C supports MFA using SMS, TOTP apps, or third-party IdPs.

Testing MFA Scenarios:

- Attempt login with and without MFA to ensure the policy enforces it.

- Attempt to bypass MFA using browser tools or request manipulation.

- Ensure the same device/browser does not skip MFA unexpectedly unless trusted devices are configured.

MFA Policy Example:

```
<OrchestrationStep Order="4" Type="ClaimsExchange">
  <ClaimsExchanges>
    <ClaimsExchange                                        Id="MFA"
TechnicalProfileReferenceId="PhoneFactor-InputOrVerify" />
  </ClaimsExchanges>
</OrchestrationStep>
```

Recommendation: Use MFA in high-privilege flows like password reset, admin sign-in, or sensitive action confirmation.

Penetration Testing Guidelines

Microsoft permits penetration testing of Azure services, including B2C, as long as you follow their rules of engagement.

1. **Register Your Test:** Although not required anymore, review Microsoft's current pen test policy at: https://learn.microsoft.com/en-us/legal/pen-testing

2. **Scope Carefully:** Only test your tenant, applications, and endpoints. Do not test Microsoft-owned infrastructure.

3. **Use Non-Production Environments:** Run all security tests in isolated, non-production B2C tenants.

4. **Document Findings:** Create a detailed report outlining any vulnerabilities, severity, and mitigation steps.

Common Misconfigurations to Avoid

Misconfiguration	Impact	Recommendation
Allowing `response_mode=form_post` on public clients	Token leakage	Use `redirect` mode in SPAs
Exposing all claims by default	Data leakage	Use `OutputClaims` selectively
Overly permissive API scopes	Unauthorized access	Define minimal custom scopes
Token lifetime too long	Increased risk on token theft	Use short lifetimes and refresh tokens
Weak passwords / no lockout policy	Brute-force vulnerability	Enforce password complexity and lockouts

Recommended Tools and Techniques

- **Application Insights**: Monitor claim values and orchestration steps.

- **Azure Monitor**: Aggregate security-related events.

- **Kusto Query Language (KQL)**: Investigate anomalies in logs.

- **OWASP ZAP / Burp Suite**: Perform manual security testing.

- **jwt.io / Fiddler / Postman**: Validate and inspect tokens and flows.

- **Azure Policy + Defender for Cloud**: Add compliance and threat protection layers.

Conclusion

Azure AD B2C provides an extremely capable and secure platform, but only when configured and tested thoroughly. Identity systems are attractive targets for attackers, and B2C's flexibility can either be a strength or a liability depending on how it's managed.

By applying a disciplined security testing strategy, validating token handling, safeguarding custom policies and REST APIs, and employing best practices across all layers of integration, you can transform Azure AD B2C into a security asset rather than a liability. Remember: in identity security, the absence of evidence is not evidence of absence—proactive testing is essential for real protection.

Chapter 9: Deployment, Scaling, and Maintenance

CI/CD Integration for Custom Policies

Integrating Continuous Integration and Continuous Deployment (CI/CD) into your Azure AD B2C custom policy development workflow is essential for managing complexity, improving consistency, and accelerating delivery. This section explores the full lifecycle of implementing a CI/CD pipeline for Azure AD B2C custom policies—from local development through to production deployment.

Overview of CI/CD in Azure AD B2C

CI/CD pipelines in Azure AD B2C primarily revolve around automating the deployment of policy files (XML), managing secrets, and safely promoting configurations across different environments such as development, testing, and production. By leveraging CI/CD, you eliminate the risks associated with manual deployments and achieve reliable policy versioning.

Key components to consider:

- Source Control Management (e.g., GitHub, Azure Repos)

- Build Agents (e.g., GitHub Actions, Azure DevOps Pipelines)

- Policy Deployment Scripts (PowerShell, Azure CLI, Bicep)

- Secret Management (Azure Key Vault)

- Environment Segmentation (via tenant separation or policy prefixes)

Organizing Your Custom Policy Repository

Organize your repository to support maintainability and promote clean integration with automation tools. A standard folder structure may look like:

```
/b2c-policies
  /base
    TrustFrameworkBase.xml
  /extensions
```

```
  TrustFrameworkExtensions.xml
 /signupsignin
   SignUpOrSignin.xml
 /passwordreset
   PasswordReset.xml
 /profileedit
   ProfileEdit.xml
 /scripts
   deploy-policy.ps1
   validate-policy.ps1
```

You may also include an env folder to hold environment-specific overrides or configurations.

Writing Deployment Scripts

A deployment script automates the upload and assignment of policy files to the Azure AD B2C tenant. The following is a simplified PowerShell script that handles policy deployment:

```
param (
    [string]$TenantName,
    [string]$ClientId,
    [string]$ClientSecret,
    [string]$PolicyFolder
)

$token    =    az    account    get-access-token    --resource
https://graph.microsoft.com/ --query accessToken -o tsv

$headers = @{
    "Authorization" = "Bearer $token"
    "Content-Type"  = "application/xml"
}

$policyFiles = Get-ChildItem -Path $PolicyFolder -Filter *.xml

foreach ($file in $policyFiles) {
    $policyName = $file.BaseName
    $content = Get-Content -Path $file.FullName -Raw
```

```
    Invoke-RestMethod                                    -Uri
"https://graph.microsoft.com/beta/trustFramework/policies/$policyNam
e/\$value" `
                    -Method PUT `
                    -Headers $headers `
                    -Body $content
}
```

This script requires Azure CLI authentication and uploads each policy file to the B2C tenant using Microsoft Graph API. In practice, consider robust error handling and logging.

GitHub Actions for CI/CD

Using GitHub Actions, you can automate policy validation and deployment. A sample workflow YAML (.github/workflows/deploy-b2c.yml) could be:

```
name: Deploy B2C Policies

on:
  push:
    branches: [main]

jobs:
  deploy:
    runs-on: ubuntu-latest

    steps:
    - name: Checkout Code
      uses: actions/checkout@v3

    - name: Azure Login
      uses: azure/login@v1
      with:
        creds: ${{ secrets.AZURE_CREDENTIALS }}

    - name: Deploy Policies
      run: |
        az account set --subscription "${{ secrets.AZURE_SUBSCRIPTION_ID }}"
```

```
    pwsh ./b2c-policies/scripts/deploy-policy.ps1 `
        -TenantName "${{ secrets.B2C_TENANT_NAME }}" `
        -ClientId "${{ secrets.B2C_CLIENT_ID }}" `
        -ClientSecret "${{ secrets.B2C_CLIENT_SECRET }}" `
        -PolicyFolder "./b2c-policies/signupsignin"
```

Secrets such as client credentials and tenant information are securely stored in GitHub Secrets and injected at runtime. You can also trigger this pipeline manually or upon pull requests for different branches.

Azure DevOps Pipeline Example

For teams using Azure DevOps, the YAML pipeline might look like:

```
trigger:
- main

pool:
  vmImage: 'ubuntu-latest'

variables:
  - group: B2CSecrets

steps:
- task: AzureCLI@2
  inputs:
    azureSubscription: 'B2C-Service-Connection'
    scriptType: 'ps'
    scriptLocation: 'inlineScript'
    inlineScript: |
      pwsh ./b2c-policies/scripts/deploy-policy.ps1 `
        -TenantName "$(B2C_TENANT_NAME)" `
        -ClientId "$(B2C_CLIENT_ID)" `
        -ClientSecret "$(B2C_CLIENT_SECRET)" `
        -PolicyFolder "./b2c-policies"
```

This integrates well with Azure Key Vault-backed variable groups for enhanced security. You can create stages such as build, validate, deploy-dev, deploy-prod for structured deployment.

234 | Mastering Azure AD B2C

Validating Policies Before Deployment

Ensure policies are syntactically correct and pass compilation before deploying. A common approach includes:

- Using custom PowerShell validation scripts

- Using Microsoft Graph to test policy upload to a non-production tenant

- Running XML schema validation

- Automating policy simulation via Microsoft's Policy Debugger (if applicable)

Example:

```
function Validate-Policy {
    param([string]$Path)

    try {
        [xml]$xml = Get-Content $Path
        Write-Host "Valid XML: $Path" -ForegroundColor Green
    } catch {
        Write-Error "Invalid XML: $Path"
        exit 1
    }
}
```

Integrate this into your GitHub Actions or Azure Pipelines for early detection of errors.

Environment Separation Strategies

Azure AD B2C does not support multiple environments natively. You can simulate this in two ways:

1. **Multiple Tenants**:
Have a `myb2ctenant-dev`, `myb2ctenant-test`, and `myb2ctenant-prod`. Each tenant holds its own policy configurations and application registrations. While this is the cleanest approach, managing multiple tenants can be administratively heavier.

2. **Policy Prefixes**:
Use different prefixes for policy files, e.g., `B2C_1A_DEV_SignUp`, `B2C_1A_PROD_SignUp`.

This allows for environment-specific flows within the same tenant. You must ensure apps are correctly linked to their corresponding policy.

Rollbacks and Version Control

Version control of policy files is critical. Git handles this effectively. A solid approach is to:

- Commit each policy change with a meaningful message

- Tag releases with semantic versioning (e.g., `v1.0.0`)

- Create release branches for production-ready policies

Additionally, you can store backups in a blob storage container or Azure Repos artifacts.

For rollback, simply redeploy a previous tagged version using your CI/CD workflow.

Security Best Practices

- **Use App Registrations with Least Privilege**: Only allow permissions necessary to manage policies (`Policy.ReadWrite.TrustFramework`).

- **Store Secrets in Secure Vaults**: Use Azure Key Vault or GitHub Encrypted Secrets.

- **Audit Policy Changes**: Use Git history and Azure Activity Logs.

- **Secure Build Agents**: Run pipelines on isolated and trusted agents to prevent secret leakage.

Conclusion

Integrating CI/CD into your Azure AD B2C custom policy workflow not only boosts team productivity but also improves overall policy governance and reliability. Whether you choose GitHub Actions, Azure DevOps, or another automation tool, the key lies in structuring your repositories, scripting your deployments, validating your changes, and promoting secure, controlled releases across your environments.

This foundational automation enables you to scale Azure AD B2C usage across multiple applications and development teams without sacrificing control or introducing unnecessary friction.

Environment Management (Dev, Test, Prod)

Effective environment management is critical when working with Azure AD B2C, especially in larger or enterprise-scale applications where development, testing, and production environments must be separated for stability, security, and compliance. This section provides an in-depth guide to managing environments when working with Azure AD B2C custom policies and applications, offering practical advice on tenant architecture, configuration separation, identity synchronization, environment automation, and best practices.

Why Environment Separation Matters

Separation of environments ensures that:

- Developers can test changes without affecting live users.

- QA teams can validate business logic and UX/UI flows independently.

- Production remains stable, secure, and compliant.

Environment management also supports CI/CD, rollback strategies, access control, and troubleshooting, by isolating risk and allowing controlled promotion of changes.

Approaches to Environment Separation in Azure AD B2C

Azure AD B2C does not natively support environment segmentation within a single tenant. Therefore, there are two primary strategies you can adopt:

1. **Multiple Azure AD B2C Tenants**

2. **Policy and App Prefixing within a Single Tenant**

Multiple Tenants Strategy

In this approach, you create a separate B2C tenant for each environment:

- **myapp-dev.b2clogin.com**

- **myapp-test.b2clogin.com**

- **myapp-prod.b2clogin.com**

Each tenant contains:

- Its own policy files

- App registrations

- Identity providers

- Branding and content definitions

This strategy provides the highest level of separation and is the recommended approach for large teams or production systems where stability and security are paramount.

Benefits:

- Absolute isolation between environments

- Minimal risk of unintentional changes in production

- Clean segregation of user data

Challenges:

- Increases management overhead

- Requires duplication of setup across tenants

- Cannot share users across environments

Setting Up Multiple Tenants

You can create and configure tenants either via the Azure portal or with Azure CLI.

Create a new tenant (via Azure CLI):

```
az ad b2c directory create --display-name "MyApp Dev Tenant" --domain-
name "myappdev.onmicrosoft.com"
```

After creation, switch your context:

```
az account tenant set --tenant <tenant-id>
```

Then, create user flows or upload custom policies as needed.

For enterprise management, you may wish to script and parameterize the setup using tools like Bicep or Terraform to maintain consistency across environments.

Policy and App Prefixing (Single Tenant Strategy)

If managing multiple tenants is too heavy or your app doesn't warrant full isolation, you can opt for using prefixes or suffixes to distinguish environments within a single tenant.

Example naming:

- Policies: `B2C_1A_DEV_SignUpOrSignIn`, `B2C_1A_PROD_SignUpOrSignIn`

- Applications: `myapp-dev,` `myapp-test,` `myapp-prod`

This strategy works well in smaller applications or where user identity does not need to be strictly isolated across environments.

To make this approach more robust:

- Assign different redirect URIs per environment

- Register separate client secrets or certificates

- Scope API permissions specifically for each app registration

Application Registration Across Environments

Each environment should have its own app registrations with environment-specific settings.

Example: Registering Apps via Azure CLI

```
az ad app create \
  --display-name "myapp-dev" \
  --reply-urls "https://localhost:3000/auth" \
  --identifier-uris "https://myapp-dev" \
  --available-to-other-tenants false
```

Then, create a service principal and assign API permissions:

```
az ad sp create --id <app-id>
az ad app permission add --id <app-id> --api <api-id> --api-
permissions <permissions>
```

Use environment-specific secrets for each:

```
az ad app credential reset --id <app-id> --append --years 1
```

Store and retrieve these secrets securely in CI/CD tools or from Azure Key Vault.

Maintaining Policy Consistency

Use version control to track and manage differences between policy files per environment. This includes:

- TrustFrameworkBase.xml

- TrustFrameworkExtensions.xml

- User flow XMLs (e.g., SignUpOrSignIn.xml)

You can use Git branches or folders like:

```
/b2c-policies
  /dev
    TrustFrameworkExtensions.xml
  /test
  /prod
```

This organization supports easy diffing, promotion, and rollback. Use pull requests to merge changes from dev → test → prod.

Tip: Use tokens or placeholders in policy XML and replace them at deployment time with environment-specific values.

Handling Identity Providers per Environment

Each environment should use separate instances or keys for external identity providers (Google, Facebook, etc.) to avoid conflicts and security risks.

For instance, register different Google apps:

- Google   Dev   App   →   for   myapp-dev.b2clogin.com

- Google   Prod   App   →   for   myapp-prod.b2clogin.com

Each app will have its own client ID and secret, which are mapped in the Identity Providers section of your B2C tenant.

External API Connectors and Claims

Custom policies may use RESTful API connectors to fetch data or perform business logic. These endpoints must be separated per environment to avoid data leakage or breaking production services with test inputs.

Example:

- Dev   endpoint: `https://api-dev.myapp.com/b2c/profile-check`

- Test   endpoint: `https://api-test.myapp.com/b2c/profile-check`

- Prod   endpoint: `https://api.myapp.com/b2c/profile-check`

Use parameters or environment variables in your deployment scripts to insert the correct API URLs.

Automating Environment Promotion

Promoting custom policies across environments can be done manually, but automation improves consistency and safety.

Example Promotion Script (PowerShell):

```
param(
    [string]$SourceFolder,
    [string]$TargetTenantId,
    [string]$TargetClientId,
```

```
    [string]$TargetSecret
)

# Login and acquire token
$token     =    az    account    get-access-token    --resource
https://graph.microsoft.com/ --query accessToken -o tsv

$headers = @{
    "Authorization" = "Bearer $token"
    "Content-Type"  = "application/xml"
}

$policyFiles = Get-ChildItem -Path $SourceFolder -Filter *.xml

foreach ($file in $policyFiles) {
    $policyName = $file.BaseName
    $content = Get-Content -Path $file.FullName -Raw
    Invoke-RestMethod                                        -Uri
"https://graph.microsoft.com/beta/trustFramework/policies/$policyNam
e/\$value" `
                    -Method PUT `
                    -Headers $headers `
                    -Body $content
}
```

Trigger this script from your CI/CD pipeline on PR merges to specific branches.

Versioning and Change Management

Use semantic versioning or date-based tagging:

- `v1.0.0-dev`

- `v1.0.0-prod`   •

- `2025-04-01-prod`

Maintain a `CHANGELOG.md` in your repository to record:

- Policy additions and removals

- API connector updates

- UI/UX changes (JavaScript, branding)

- MFA and identity provider changes

Ensure stakeholders and QA teams sign off on changes before promoting to production.

Monitoring and Alerting per Environment

Enable Application Insights or Log Analytics in each environment to capture:

- Sign-in success/failure metrics

- API connector response codes

- Exception traces

- Custom event logs

This provides telemetry to isolate bugs and measure user flow performance.

In production, consider setting up alerts:

- Failed logins > threshold

- High latency on token issuance

- API connector downtime

Integrate monitoring dashboards with tools like Azure Monitor, Grafana, or Power BI.

Environment Governance

To enforce correct usage of environments, apply the following practices:

- **Access Control**: Use Role-Based Access Control (RBAC) to restrict who can change settings in each tenant.

- **Audit Logs**: Enable and monitor audit logs to track configuration changes.

- **Policy Locking**: Freeze the production branch except via approved release processes.

- **Secret Rotation**: Periodically rotate app secrets and certificates and store them securely.

Conclusion

Environment management in Azure AD B2C requires deliberate architecture, especially when using custom policies and multiple integrated applications. By establishing separate environments—either via multiple tenants or strict prefixing within a single tenant—you enable safer, more predictable development and release workflows.

Combined with automated deployment scripts, strict governance, and robust monitoring, this approach ensures your Azure AD B2C solution remains scalable, secure, and maintainable throughout its lifecycle. Environment management is the backbone of modern DevSecOps in identity management, and getting it right pays dividends in agility and risk mitigation.

Backup, Version Control, and Policy Auditing

In any system handling authentication and identity, maintaining reliable backups, strong version control practices, and thorough audit trails is essential. Azure AD B2C custom policies are no exception. Because policies in B2C control user journeys, authentication methods, API connectors, and claims transformations, even small changes can significantly impact functionality and user experience. This section explores how to implement a robust backup, versioning, and auditing strategy for custom policies and related resources in Azure AD B2C.

Why Backup and Version Control Matter

Custom policies are written in XML and uploaded to the B2C tenant via the Azure portal or automation scripts. These files represent the "code" of your identity system and should be treated just like any other software artifact:

- **Backups** protect against accidental deletion or corruption.

- **Version control** enables safe collaboration, change tracking, and rollback.

- **Auditing** supports compliance, security review, and operational transparency.

Without these practices, you risk losing critical configuration, deploying broken flows to production, or being unable to trace changes in the event of failure or breach.

Structuring Your Repository for Version Control

Using Git is the standard for versioning custom policy XML files. Organize your repo with clarity and scalability in mind:

```
/b2c-policies
  /base
    TrustFrameworkBase.xml
  /extensions
    TrustFrameworkExtensions.xml
  /userflows
    SignUpOrSignIn.xml
    PasswordReset.xml
    ProfileEdit.xml
  /env
    /dev
    /test
    /prod
  /scripts
    deploy-policies.ps1
    validate-policies.ps1
  changelog.md
  README.md
```

Each folder contains files related to that component. The `env` folder allows for environment-specific overrides or policy references. `scripts` holds your automation tools, while the changelog documents human-readable updates.

Version Control Practices

Follow modern Git practices to ensure smooth collaboration and traceability:

- **Branches**: Use `main` for production-ready policies, `dev` for current development, and feature branches for major changes.

- **Commits**: Write clear, descriptive commit messages (`feat: add MFA claims to sign-in policy`).

- **Tags**: Create tags for releases (`v1.0.0`, `v2.1.0-prod`) so you can revert quickly.

- **Pull Requests**: Use PRs to review and discuss changes before merging. Include links to policy documentation and test cases.

Example: Creating a tag for a stable policy release

```
git checkout main
git tag -a v1.2.0 -m "Stable release of MFA policies for production"
git push origin v1.2.0
```

Example: Rolling back to a previous tag

```
git checkout tags/v1.1.0
./scripts/deploy-policies.ps1 -Environment prod
```

Storing and Archiving Backups

In addition to Git, you should archive deployed versions of your policies in a secure, tamper-proof location—especially for production.

Options include:

- Azure Blob Storage with versioning
- GitHub Releases with ZIP archives
- Azure DevOps Artifacts
- External backup systems (e.g., AWS S3, Google Drive for small teams)

Example: Archiving to Azure Blob Storage using Azure CLI

```
az storage blob upload-batch \
  --destination b2cbackups \
  --source ./b2c-policies \
```

```
--account-name mystorageaccount \
--pattern *.xml
```

To support versioning, include the commit hash or tag in the storage path:

```
--destination-path "v1.3.0/"
```

Automation Tip: Add backup steps to your CI/CD pipeline before deploying any policy to test or production environments.

Automating Backup and Version History with CI/CD

You can configure your pipeline to automatically archive policy files on every merge to `main` or before each deployment.

GitHub Actions Example:

```
name: Backup and Deploy B2C Policies

on:
  push:
    branches: [main]

jobs:
  backup-and-deploy:
    runs-on: ubuntu-latest
    steps:
      - uses: actions/checkout@v3

      - name: Archive Policy Files
        run: |
          zip -r policies-$(date +%Y%m%d%H%M%S).zip ./b2c-policies

      - name: Upload to Azure Blob
        run: |
          az storage blob upload \
            --file ./policies-*.zip \
            --container-name b2cbackups \
            --name policies-$(date +%Y%m%d%H%M%S).zip \
```

```
    --account-name mystorageaccount
```

You can also publish a GitHub release for manual downloads.

Policy Change Auditing

In production environments, you need to track not just *what* changed, but also *who* changed it and *why*.

Ways to audit policy changes:

1. **Git   Commit   History**
   Git   tracks   author,   timestamp,   and   commit   message.

Azure   Activity   Logs
In Azure, activity logs capture actions like uploading policies via the portal or API.

View   logs   via   Azure   CLI:

bash

```
az monitor activity-log list --resource-group <your-rg>
```
Or   export   them   to   Log   Analytics   for   querying   and   alerting:

kusto

```
AzureActivity
| where ResourceProvider == "Microsoft.AzureActiveDirectory"
| where ActivityStatus == "Succeeded"
| where OperationName contains "TrustFrameworkPolicy"
```

2.

Manual   Change   Logs
Maintain a `CHANGELOG.md` file that describes each update in human-readable form:

markdown

```
## [1.2.0] - 2025-04-01
### Added
- New custom MFA claims in SignUpOrSignIn.xml
- REST API connector for license check
```

```
### Changed
- Updated branding HTML for accessibility
```

3.
4. **CI/CD**   **Audit**   **Trail**
   Most pipeline tools log who triggered a deployment and from which commit hash. Retain this data for at least 6–12 months.

Validating Backups and Restores

Backups are only useful if you can restore them reliably.

Test your backup strategy by:

- Restoring older policies to a test tenant

- Using `diff` tools to compare restored versions with live production

- Running automated tests or manual sign-ins through flows after restore

Example PowerShell Restore Script:

```
param(
    [string]$BackupPath,
    [string]$TenantName,
    [string]$ClientId,
    [string]$ClientSecret
)

$files = Get-ChildItem -Path $BackupPath -Filter *.xml

foreach ($file in $files) {
    Write-Host "Restoring policy: $($file.Name)"
    # Call upload logic here...
}
```

Integrating with Policy Testing Pipelines

As part of backup verification, you can integrate basic policy tests such as:

- Checking for well-formed XML
- Ensuring required policy references exist
- Verifying that token issuance still works

Automated tools or custom scripts can check for:

- XML syntax errors
- Broken `<TechnicalProfile>` references
- Missing content definitions
- Invalid API connector URLs

Long-Term Retention and Compliance

For organizations under regulatory oversight, long-term retention of policy versions is often required for audits or forensic investigations.

Recommendations:

- Retain at least 12–24 months of policy changes
- Store backups in multiple regions or cloud providers
- Encrypt archived backups
- Log access to backup locations
- Periodically test recovery procedures

Best Practices Summary

- **Always version your policy changes using Git.**
- **Automate backups before each deployment.**
- **Use tags and changelogs to mark stable releases.**

- **Store backups in secure, redundant locations.**
- **Audit changes via Git, Azure logs, and CI/CD tools.**
- **Test restores regularly in sandbox environments.**
- **Encrypt and protect all stored policy files and secrets.**

Conclusion

A mature Azure AD B2C deployment depends not just on writing solid policies, but also on how you manage them over time. By implementing strong backup, version control, and auditing practices, you ensure operational stability, traceability, and compliance. These processes also empower your team to iterate confidently, deploy safely, and recover quickly when needed. Treat your policies as code, and you'll unlock the full potential of identity as a managed service.

Monitoring Performance and Reliability

Ensuring the performance and reliability of Azure AD B2C custom policies and associated identity infrastructure is crucial to delivering a seamless, secure, and scalable user experience. Identity is often the front door to your application, and any latency, error, or downtime directly impacts user trust and business continuity. This section explores monitoring strategies, performance tuning, telemetry collection, error diagnostics, and proactive reliability practices for Azure AD B2C.

The Importance of Monitoring in Identity Systems

Azure AD B2C is responsible for:

- Authenticating users
- Issuing secure tokens
- Handling multi-factor authentication (MFA)
- Calling API connectors
- Managing user flows and custom journeys

A single misconfiguration or performance issue can cause:

- Slow login experiences
- Failed authentications
- Token issuance delays
- Downtime in critical user-facing systems

Monitoring ensures you're alerted to issues before users are, and allows teams to analyze, respond to, and prevent future incidents.

Key Metrics to Monitor

To assess performance and reliability, focus on the following categories:

1. **Authentication** **Metrics**
   - Average response time for user flows
   - Token issuance latency
   - Login success vs. failure rates
   - MFA challenges triggered and completed

2. **Policy** **Execution** **Metrics**
   - Execution time for custom policies
   - REST API connector latency and failures
   - TechnicalProfile resolution errors
   - Session handling timeouts

3. **System** **Health** **Metrics**
   - HTTP error rates (4xx, 5xx)
   - Azure service availability
   - Application Insights availability tests
   - Throttling incidents

4. **User** **Experience** **Metrics**

- ○ Drop-off rates in sign-up or sign-in journeys
- ○ Error page impressions
- ○ Localization fallback errors

Setting Up Application Insights for Azure AD B2C

Azure AD B2C supports integrating with **Application Insights**, allowing you to collect telemetry during custom policy execution. This is enabled via the `InstrumentationKey` in your policy XML.

Step 1: Create an Application Insights Resource

In the Azure portal:

- Navigate to *Application Insights*
- Create a new resource in the same region as your B2C tenant
- Copy the Instrumentation Key (or Connection String)

Step 2: Add Application Insights to TrustFrameworkExtensions.xml

In your policy file, add or update the `<Diagnostics>` node:

```
<BuildingBlocks>
  <Diagnostics>
    <InstrumentationKey>YOUR-INSTRUMENTATION-
KEY</InstrumentationKey>
  </Diagnostics>
</BuildingBlocks>
```

Telemetry from custom policy execution will now be routed to Application Insights, including:

- User journey steps
- Errors

- Latency

- API   call   outcomes

Querying Telemetry Data

Use Kusto Query Language (KQL) to query data in Application Insights. Examples:

Sign-in policy execution errors:

```
traces
| where message contains "Exception"
| where customDimensions["PolicyId"] == "B2C_1A_SIGNIN"
| project timestamp, message, customDimensions
```

Latency of API connector calls:

```
requests
| where name contains "api-connector"
| summarize avg(duration) by name
```

Token issuance failures:

```
traces
| where message contains "Token issuance failed"
| project timestamp, user_Id, message
```

User journey timeline:

```
traces
| where customDimensions contains "JourneyRecorder"
| order by timestamp asc
```

Use dashboards to visualize these queries and detect trends or anomalies.

Implementing Availability Monitoring

You can simulate user flow execution using **Application Insights Availability Tests** to monitor performance and reliability:

1. Navigate to your Application Insights instance
2. Go to **Availability** > **Add** **Test**
3. Configure:

   - Type: URL Ping Test
   - URL:
     https://yourtenant.b2clogin.com/yourtenant.onmicrosoft.com/B2C_1A_SIGNIN/oauth2/v2.0/authorize?...
   - Test frequency: every 5 minutes
   - Locations: select multiple regions

These synthetic tests simulate real user traffic and alert you to issues before customers notice them.

Tip: Monitor all production policies, including sign-in, sign-up, and password reset.

Diagnosing Issues with Policy Execution

Azure AD B2C provides built-in error reporting in the UI, but for deeper diagnostics, enable logging in your policies.

Enable verbose logging:

In <TrustFrameworkPolicy>, enable journey recorder:

```
<ClaimsTransformation                                      Id="LogStep"
TransformationMethod="FormatString">
  <InputClaims>
    <InputClaim                         ClaimTypeReferenceId="step"
TransformationClaimType="inputClaim1" />
  </InputClaims>
  <InputParameters>
```

```
    <InputParameter          Id="stringFormat">Policy          Step:
{0}</InputParameter>
  </InputParameters>
  <OutputClaims>
    <OutputClaim              ClaimTypeReferenceId="debugMessage"
TransformationClaimType="outputClaim" />
  </OutputClaims>
</ClaimsTransformation>
```

Route the debugMessage to Application Insights or display it in error pages for debugging.

REST API Connector Monitoring

RESTful API connectors are commonly used in custom policies. Monitoring their performance and error rates is vital.

Best Practices:

- Enable logging on your APIs (App Insights, Serilog, ELK, etc.)

- Log correlation IDs (x-correlation-id) for traceability

- Track:

  ○ Request duration

  ○ HTTP status codes

  ○ Payload validation failures

Log example (server-side):

```
{
  "timestamp": "2025-04-02T12:00:00Z",
  "event": "UserProfileValidation",
  "status": 200,
  "responseTimeMs": 350,
  "userId": "abc123",
  "correlationId": "xyz-456"
}
```

Client-side telemetry in B2C (via KQL):

```
requests
| where url contains "profile-check"
| summarize avg(duration), count() by resultCode
```

Set alerts on high latency or increased 5xx responses to detect failures early.

Performance Optimization Techniques

Monitoring highlights bottlenecks. To improve performance, apply these techniques:

- **Reduce Policy Complexity:** Avoid over-nesting of `OrchestrationStep` elements. Simplify technical profiles where possible.

- **Avoid Redundant API Calls:** Combine multiple API connectors into one where practical.

- **Use Caching:** Store frequently-used data in claims or external cache (e.g., Redis, Azure Cache for Redis).

- **Optimize Token Sizes:** Remove unused claims and custom attributes.

- **Parallel Execution:** Run non-dependent orchestration steps in separate journeys.

Each change should be measured using performance metrics before and after deployment.

Reliability Engineering in B2C

To ensure ongoing reliability:

- **Implement Circuit Breakers** in external APIs to avoid cascading failures.

- **Fail Gracefully:** Configure `ErrorMessage` claims for known failure types.

- **Test Load Scenarios:** Use tools like Azure Load Testing or JMeter.

- **Scale API Connectors:** Ensure APIs used by policies are horizontally scalable.

Proactive Alerting and Incident Management

Set up alerts for:

- Token issuance failure rate > 2%
- REST API latency > 2s
- MFA drop-off rate > 5%
- 5xx errors in availability tests

Azure Monitor Alert Example:

```
{
  "condition": {
    "metricName": "availabilityResults/availabilityPercentage",
    "operator": "LessThan",
    "threshold": 95
  },
  "actionGroups": ["email-oncall", "sms-devops"]
}
```

Configure alerts to trigger automated incident response playbooks or create tickets in systems like PagerDuty or ServiceNow.

SLA Monitoring and Reporting

Define internal SLAs for identity services. Example:

Metric	Target
Avg. login response time	< 1 second
REST API success rate	> 99.9%
MFA challenge success rate	> 98%
Token issuance failure rate	< 0.1%

Generate monthly reports using Power BI or Excel integrated with Application Insights or Azure Monitor Workbooks.

Conclusion

Monitoring performance and reliability in Azure AD B2C is a multidimensional effort, spanning policy execution, user experience, external API integrations, and service availability. By integrating Application Insights, setting up synthetic monitoring, and leveraging alerts and diagnostics, you gain visibility and control over the entire identity lifecycle.

This visibility enables you to respond to incidents quickly, optimize user journeys, and deliver a stable authentication experience at scale. Treating your identity flows as production-grade applications ensures that authentication isn't just functional—it's fast, reliable, and resilient.

Chapter 10: Real-World Scenarios and Best Practices

Implementing B2C in E-commerce Applications

In the competitive world of e-commerce, user experience and security are paramount. Azure Active Directory B2C (Azure AD B2C) offers an identity management solution tailored for customer-facing applications, making it an excellent choice for e-commerce platforms that need to scale securely while offering seamless login experiences across devices and channels.

This section dives deep into implementing Azure AD B2C in an e-commerce context, covering practical steps, architecture recommendations, customization strategies, and best practices.

Key Identity Requirements in E-commerce

E-commerce applications often have distinct identity requirements that Azure AD B2C is well-suited to address:

- **Scalable User Base**: Ability to support millions of users globally.

- **Multiple Authentication Methods**: Support for local accounts, social logins (Google, Facebook, etc.), and possibly federated enterprise logins for B2B2C scenarios.

- **Custom Branding and UX**: Fully tailored login, sign-up, and password reset experiences.

- **High Security**: Protection from identity fraud, account takeover, and other threats.

- **Compliance**: Support for regulations like GDPR, CCPA.

Architecture Overview

At a high level, the architecture for using Azure AD B2C in an e-commerce platform typically involves:

1. **Frontend**: SPA (React, Angular, Vue) or server-rendered pages (Next.js, ASP.NET MVC) with B2C login integration.

2. **Backend APIs**: Secured by validating access tokens issued by Azure AD B2C.

3. **B2C Tenant**: Configured with identity providers, user flows, custom policies, branding, and extensions as needed.

Here is a sample architecture flow:

1. User visits the e-commerce site.

2. The site initiates a login flow using Azure AD B2C.

3. B2C authenticates the user (via local or social account).

4. The user receives an ID and access token.

5. The token is sent with requests to backend APIs for authentication and authorization.

Registering the Application

To begin integrating Azure AD B2C, register your application in the Azure portal:

1. Navigate to your B2C tenant in the Azure portal.

2. Go to **App registrations** > **New registration**.

3. Name your app (e.g., MyEcommerceWeb).

4. Choose the appropriate platform (SPA or web).

5. Add a redirect URI (e.g., https://myecommerce.com/auth/callback).

6. Record the Application (client) ID for later use.

For SPAs:

```
// Example redirect URIs for SPAs

{

  "redirectUris": [

    "https://myecommerce.com/auth/callback"

  ],

  "implicitGrantSettings": {

    "enableIdTokenIssuance": true,
```

```
    "enableAccessTokenIssuance": true

  }

}
```

Setting Up User Flows

Choose between built-in user flows and custom policies based on your complexity needs.

For most e-commerce apps, **user flows** provide sufficient flexibility:

- **Sign up and sign in**: Create a unified flow.

- **Password reset**: Ensure users can reset forgotten passwords.

- **Profile editing**: Allow users to update their info.

Create these from **User flows** in the Azure portal. Configure attributes (e.g., email, displayName) and claims to match your user database schema.

Custom Branding

Branding is critical in e-commerce to maintain trust and consistency.

1. Upload your logo.

2. Customize the layout using HTML templates.

3. Inject custom CSS to match your theme.

4. Use JavaScript for validation or UI tweaks (e.g., show/hide fields).

```
<style>

  body {

    background-color: #f8f8f8;

    font-family: 'Segoe UI', sans-serif;

  }
```

```css
.banner {

  background-color: #2e3b4e;

  color: #fff;

  padding: 10px;

}
```

```
</style>
```

```html
<script type="text/javascript">

  document.addEventListener('DOMContentLoaded', function() {

    const emailInput = document.getElementById('email');

    if (emailInput) {

      emailInput.placeholder = 'Enter your email to get started';

    }

  });

</script>
```

Integrating with Your Web App

Use Microsoft Authentication Library (MSAL) for JavaScript or your framework's library (e.g., @azure/msal-browser for React).

Sample configuration:

```javascript
const msalConfig = {

  auth: {

    clientId: 'your-client-id',
```

```
    authority:
'https://yourtenant.b2clogin.com/yourtenant.onmicrosoft.com/B2C_1_si
gnupsignin',

    redirectUri: 'https://myecommerce.com/auth/callback'

  },

  cache: {

    cacheLocation: 'localStorage',

    storeAuthStateInCookie: true

  }

};
```

Use `loginRedirect` or `loginPopup` to initiate the login flow:

```
const msalInstance = new PublicClientApplication(msalConfig);


function signIn() {

  msalInstance.loginRedirect();

}
```

Token Validation on Backend

When users interact with secured APIs (e.g., checkout, view orders), your backend must validate the JWT access tokens issued by B2C.

For Node.js (Express) with `passport-azure-ad`:

```
const BearerStrategy = require('passport-azure-ad').BearerStrategy;
```

```
const options = {

  identityMetadata:
`https://login.microsoftonline.com/yourtenant.onmicrosoft.com/v2.0/.
well-known/openid-configuration?p=B2C_1_signupsignin`,

  clientID: 'your-client-id',

  policyName: 'B2C_1_signupsignin',

  isB2C: true,

  validateIssuer: true,

  loggingLevel: 'info',

  passReqToCallback: false

};


passport.use(new BearerStrategy(options, (token, done) => {

  return done(null, token);

}));
```

In .NET (ASP.NET Core):

```
services.AddAuthentication(AzureADB2CDefaults.BearerAuthenticationSc
heme)

    .AddAzureADB2CBearer(options => Configuration.Bind("AzureAdB2C",
options));
```

Multi-Factor Authentication

Enable MFA via Conditional Access or directly in your user flow configuration.

- Can require MFA on all sign-ins or under specific conditions (e.g., high-value transactions).

- SMS and Authenticator app are supported.

GDPR and Consent Management

To comply with regulations:

- Capture consent explicitly during registration.
- Allow users to manage personal data and delete accounts.
- Document and disclose data usage clearly in terms of service and privacy policy.

Performance Considerations

- Use **custom domains** (e.g., `login.myecommerce.com`) to avoid redirect confusion.
- Enable **session management** for shorter or longer sign-in durations as appropriate.
- Cache tokens on client-side securely to reduce redundant logins.

Sample Use Case Flow

1. User visits site and adds items to cart.
2. At checkout, the user is prompted to sign in or sign up.
3. Azure AD B2C presents a branded sign-in page.
4. User logs in with Google.
5. User completes checkout; backend verifies token for order processing.
6. User receives order confirmation and remains signed in for future visits.

Lessons from the Field

- **Pre-fill known fields**: When users sign in via social accounts, pre-fill forms using claims like `email`, `givenName`.

- **Track user behavior**: Use `Application Insights` or Google Analytics to correlate login events with shopping behavior.

- **Optimize sign-up**: Keep the registration flow as short as possible to minimize cart abandonment.

- **Use REST API connectors**: To validate phone numbers or check for fraud before completing sign-up.

Conclusion

Implementing Azure AD B2C in e-commerce applications enables secure, scalable, and customizable identity management while improving the user experience. By leveraging user flows, social logins, branding, API protection, and compliance capabilities, you can build a seamless and trustworthy authentication journey that supports growth and customer satisfaction.

In the next section, we'll explore how B2C fits into SaaS platforms and the additional considerations needed for tenant isolation and external integrations.

B2C for SaaS Platforms

SaaS (Software-as-a-Service) platforms demand flexible, secure, and multi-tenant-capable identity solutions. Azure AD B2C provides the building blocks needed to implement identity across diverse customer organizations, ranging from startups to large enterprises. Unlike internal identity systems, SaaS identity systems must balance self-service registration, seamless sign-in, delegated admin roles, branding, scalability, and compliance — all of which Azure AD B2C supports natively or through custom extensibility.

This section explores how to leverage Azure AD B2C effectively within a SaaS architecture. We will cover design patterns, tenant models, identity federation, role-based access control, branding per customer, and enterprise readiness.

Core Identity Requirements for SaaS

A SaaS platform typically needs to solve the following identity-related challenges:

- **Multi-Tenant Support**: Customers (tenants) should be isolated logically and have their own users.

- **Delegated Administration**: Tenant admins must manage their own users without seeing other tenants' data.

- **Flexible Sign-In Options**: Support for email/password, enterprise identity providers (like Azure AD), and social logins.

- **Custom Branding**: Each tenant may require branded sign-in experiences.

- **Security**: Tenant boundaries must be strictly enforced at both identity and authorization layers.

- **Scalability**: Identity system must handle spikes in traffic and onboard new tenants without friction.

Azure AD B2C enables these capabilities when configured properly and paired with the correct backend authorization strategies.

Choosing a Tenant Model

There are two common approaches for SaaS applications when integrating Azure AD B2C:

1. Single B2C Tenant (Recommended for Most SaaS Apps)

All customers share the same Azure AD B2C tenant. Logical tenant isolation is implemented in your application and database layer.

Advantages:

- Simpler to manage and maintain.

- Easier to roll out features across all customers.

- Centralized user flows and policies.

Considerations:

- Requires robust tenant metadata tracking.

- App layer must enforce tenant-based authorization.

2. B2C Tenant per Customer (Rare Use Case)

Each customer has their own B2C tenant, typically used in regulated industries.

Advantages:

- Physical isolation of identity infrastructure.

- Custom policies and branding per customer.

Considerations:

- Complex to manage at scale.

- Harder to maintain consistent policy rollout.

Most SaaS applications should begin with the single-tenant model unless strict regulatory requirements dictate otherwise.

User Registration and Tenant Association

When a user signs up, your system must link them to the correct customer tenant context. There are multiple ways to implement this:

Option A: Invite-Based Registration

Only admins can invite users. The invite contains a tenant-specific token or link.

```
// Example: Invite link containing a tenant code

https://saasapp.com/signup?tenant=contoso
```

The application extracts the tenant code from the query string, maps it to the internal tenant ID, and stores this relationship in the user metadata after registration.

Option B: Self-Service Sign-Up with Domain Mapping

Users sign up with their email, and your app maps the domain to a tenant.

```
function getTenantFromEmail(email) {

  const domain = email.split('@')[1];

  return tenantLookupTable[domain];

}
```

Store tenant metadata in a separate table:

Tenant ID	Name	Domain	Logo URL

| 1 | Contoso | contoso.com | /branding/contoso.png |
| 2 | Fabrikam | fabrikam.net | /branding/fabrikam.svg |

After sign-up, associate the user with the appropriate tenant and enforce tenant-based access in the app.

Role-Based Access Control (RBAC)

Azure AD B2C does not include a built-in RBAC system, so you need to implement one in your application or backend.

A recommended structure:

Roles Table

Role ID	Name
1	Admin
2	Manager
3	End User

UserRoles Table

User ID	Role ID	Tenant ID
42	1	1

When a user signs in, include their role and tenant claims in the token. This can be achieved via Azure AD B2C custom policies or by enriching the token via a REST API claims provider.

Example Claim Injection

```
<ClaimsTransformation                           Id="AddCustomClaims"
TransformationMethod="CallRestfulProvider">

  <InputClaims>

    <InputClaim                       ClaimTypeReferenceId="email"
PartnerClaimType="email" />

  </InputClaims>

  <OutputClaims>

    <OutputClaim ClaimTypeReferenceId="role" PartnerClaimType="role"
/>

    <OutputClaim                      ClaimTypeReferenceId="tenant"
PartnerClaimType="tenant" />

  </OutputClaims>

</ClaimsTransformation>
```

Branding Per Customer

Azure AD B2C supports **custom domains** and **custom UI templates**. To present different branding per tenant:

1. Use a REST claims provider to look up branding based on the user's email domain or query string.

2. Inject branding info into claims.

3. Use JavaScript/CSS to dynamically render logos, colors, etc.

Sample Branding Flow

- User navigates to `https://login.saasapp.com/?tenant=contoso`

- Custom policy reads tenant from query string.

- REST API returns logo URL and color scheme.

- JavaScript renders branding on the page.

```
document.addEventListener("DOMContentLoaded", function () {

  const branding = JSON.parse(localStorage.getItem('branding'));

  if (branding) {

    document.getElementById("logo").src = branding.logoUrl;

    document.body.style.backgroundColor = branding.primaryColor;

  }

});
```

Federation with Enterprise Identity Providers

Many SaaS customers prefer to use their existing identity provider (e.g., Azure AD, Okta) to sign in.

Azure AD B2C supports this via **custom identity providers** using OpenID Connect or SAML.

Steps to Federate with Azure AD:

1. Create an enterprise application in the customer's Azure AD tenant.

2. Share your metadata URI (e.g., https://yourb2c.b2clogin.com/yourb2c.onmicrosoft.com/v2.0/.well-known/openid-configuration)

3. In your B2C tenant, add a new identity provider using the customer's OpenID Connect configuration.

Then, use a custom policy or JavaScript on your sign-in page to route the user to the correct identity provider.

```
if (email.endsWith("@contoso.com")) {

  // Redirect to Azure AD sign-in
```

```
window.location.href                                          =
"https://yourb2c.b2clogin.com/.../oauth2/v2.0/authorize?p=AzureAD_Co
ntoso";

}
```

Security and Data Isolation

In SaaS, it's critical to enforce strict boundaries between tenants. Azure AD B2C handles authentication, but authorization must be enforced in your app and API layer.

Recommendations:

- Use tenant-specific claims (`tenantId`) in access tokens.

- Filter all data queries by tenant ID.

- Log and audit access attempts across tenants.

Example API validation:

```
function validateRequest(req, res, next) {

  const userTenant = req.user.tenantId;

  const requestedTenant = req.params.tenantId;


  if (userTenant !== requestedTenant) {

    return res.status(403).send("Access denied");

  }


  next();

}
```

Subscription and Billing Integration

To tie identity with billing, track which user belongs to which subscription tier.

When a user signs in:

- Fetch their subscription level from your billing database.
- Add claims like `subscriptionLevel` to their token.
- Control feature access in the UI/backend accordingly.

Monitoring and Insights

Use **Application Insights** to track:

- Sign-up conversion rates per tenant.
- Sign-in success/failure trends.
- Identity provider usage.

```
appInsights.trackEvent({

  name: "SignInSuccess",

  properties: {

    tenantId: "contoso",

    identityProvider: "Google"

  }

});
```

Compliance and Consent

Ensure GDPR/CCPA compliance by:

- Capturing marketing consent at registration.

- Providing a data export/delete endpoint.

- Logging all consent-related events.

Store consent data in your database:

User ID	Consent Type	Given On
123	Email Marketing	2025-01-15 12:00

Best Practices Summary

- Use a single B2C tenant with tenant-aware claims for most SaaS apps.

- Use REST API claims providers to inject tenant, role, and branding info.

- Secure APIs by validating tenant context and user roles.

- Offer federated sign-in for enterprise customers.

- Leverage Application Insights for observability and metrics.

- Ensure every user action is tied to a tenant and auditable.

Final Thoughts

Azure AD B2C is a powerful, flexible identity platform for SaaS applications. By thoughtfully architecting tenant association, branding, federation, and access control, you can provide a secure and personalized experience for each of your customers. This reduces friction, enhances trust, and positions your SaaS platform for long-term success.

In the next section, we'll examine the regulatory and compliance considerations that affect B2C deployments, including GDPR, CCPA, and SOC 2 alignment.

Compliance Considerations (GDPR, CCPA)

Regulatory compliance is a foundational aspect of any modern identity solution, especially in customer-facing applications. Azure AD B2C plays a critical role in helping organizations comply with privacy regulations such as the General Data Protection Regulation (GDPR), the California Consumer Privacy Act (CCPA), and others like HIPAA, SOC 2, and ISO 27001.

This section explores how Azure AD B2C aligns with common compliance requirements, how to implement privacy-first user journeys, and how to meet obligations around user consent, data protection, rights management, auditability, and breach notifications.

Understanding Compliance in Identity Systems

When dealing with regulations such as GDPR and CCPA, identity systems become key enforcement points for:

- **User consent and preference management**
- **Right to access, modify, or delete personal data**
- **Auditability and logging of user interactions**
- **Notification and response to breaches**
- **Limiting data collection to what is necessary**

Azure AD B2C helps with these goals by offering flexible policy control, extensible user journeys, and secure, scalable identity storage hosted within Microsoft's global infrastructure that meets multiple industry certifications.

Key GDPR and CCPA Concepts Relevant to Identity

Data Subject Rights

- **Right to Access**: Users can request a copy of all data held about them.
- **Right to Rectification**: Users can update their personal information.
- **Right to Be Forgotten**: Users can request account and data deletion.
- **Right to Data Portability**: Users may ask for their data in a machine-readable format.
- **Right to Object**: Users can object to processing, including marketing.

Data Controller vs. Data Processor

- Your SaaS company is the **Data Controller**.
- Azure (Microsoft) acts as the **Data Processor** under standard contractual clauses.

You are responsible for configuring Azure AD B2C to meet your obligations, while Microsoft ensures the platform meets industry standards.

Consent Management

User consent is central to compliance. Azure AD B2C allows you to create custom user journeys that prompt for consent explicitly and store user preferences.

Example: Adding a Marketing Consent Checkbox

1. Extend your sign-up user flow or custom policy to include a new boolean claim:

```
<ClaimType Id="marketingConsent">

  <DisplayName>Marketing Consent</DisplayName>

  <DataType>boolean</DataType>

  <DefaultPartnerClaimTypes>

    <Protocol Name="OAuth2" PartnerClaimType="marketing_consent" />

  </DefaultPartnerClaimTypes>

  <UserHelpText>Do you agree to receive marketing
emails?</UserHelpText>

</ClaimType>
```

2. Update the sign-up UI page to display the checkbox:

```
<label>

  <input type="checkbox" id="marketingConsent"
name="marketingConsent">

  I agree to receive marketing emails

</label>
```

3. Store the claim in the directory or use a RESTful API connector to persist it in an external system.

This creates an audit trail for consent that can be retrieved during user data requests.

Right to Access and Export

You must provide a way for users to retrieve all personal information stored about them. This includes not only identity data (email, display name) but also linked metadata and roles stored in your application's database.

Steps:

1. Build a secure user portal with an export data feature.

2. Query Azure AD B2C via Microsoft Graph API to retrieve user information.

Sample Microsoft Graph API Call

```
GET https://graph.microsoft.com/v1.0/users/{userId}

Authorization: Bearer {access_token}
```

You must request the proper `Directory.Read.All` permission and ensure your app has admin consent.

3. Merge identity data with internal data (orders, settings) into a downloadable format (JSON, CSV, PDF).

Right to Deletion (Forget Me)

Deleting a user from Azure AD B2C can be done via:

Microsoft Graph API

```
DELETE https://graph.microsoft.com/v1.0/users/{userId}

Authorization: Bearer {access_token}
```

Ensure you also delete:

- Claims stored externally (marketing consent, preferences).
- Application-specific data (orders, logs).
- Any backups or cache that may retain personally identifiable information.

Best practice: Log deletion requests and confirmations for audit purposes.

Limiting Data Collection

Under GDPR and CCPA, you should only collect data that is strictly necessary. Avoid overloading your sign-up forms with non-essential fields.

Use Azure AD B2C's user flow configuration to control which attributes are collected during registration.

Minimal Sign-Up Flow Example

- Email address (required)
- Display name (optional)
- Marketing consent (optional)

```
<OrchestrationStep Order="1" Type="ClaimsExchange">

  <ClaimsExchanges>

    <ClaimsExchange                         Id="SignUpWithEmail"
TechnicalProfileReferenceId="SelfAsserted-LocalAccountSignUp" />

  </ClaimsExchanges>

</OrchestrationStep>
```

Avoid collecting:

- Birth date (unless required)
- Gender

- Phone number (unless used for MFA)

Be transparent about why each field is collected and how it will be used.

Data Localization and Residency

Azure AD B2C stores identity data in specific Azure regions. You can choose your region when creating the B2C tenant. This is crucial for:

- GDPR compliance (data must remain within the EU for EU users)
- Industry-specific regulations (e.g., German privacy laws)

Ensure your selected region aligns with your users' location and any local laws.

Logging and Auditing

Use **Azure AD B2C Audit Logs** and **Application Insights** to log key identity events, such as:

- Successful logins
- Failed attempts
- Account lockouts
- Consent capture
- Password resets

Set up log retention and export policies to comply with audit requirements. Logs can be exported to Azure Log Analytics or a SIEM system.

Sample Log Query (Kusto)

```
SigninLogs
| where UserPrincipalName contains "user@domain.com"
| project TimeGenerated, UserPrincipalName, AppDisplayName, Status
```

Regularly review access logs and perform anomaly detection to identify potential breaches.

Breach Notification Readiness

Azure provides strong protections at the infrastructure level, but breaches may still occur at the application level. You are responsible for:

- Detecting breaches via logs and monitoring

- Notifying authorities and affected users within regulatory timeframes (e.g., 72 hours for GDPR)

- Maintaining an incident response plan

Create a policy that defines:

- Notification templates

- Contact details for regulatory bodies

- Roles and responsibilities

Data Portability

Allow users to export their identity data in a structured, machine-readable format.

```
{

  "id": "user-123",

  "email": "user@example.com",

  "displayName": "Jane Doe",

  "marketingConsent": true,

  "roles": ["Admin"],

  "tenantId": "contoso"

}
```

Ensure the export includes only data related to the user requesting it, and is delivered securely (e.g., encrypted ZIP via email link with expiry).

Children's Data and COPPA

If your platform targets users under 13, comply with COPPA and similar laws:

- Avoid collecting personal data unless necessary.

- Get verifiable parental consent.

- Segment user journeys for minors vs. adults.

Use custom user flows to enforce age gates or use REST APIs to validate ages during registration.

Best Practices for Compliance

- Use Azure AD B2C's extensibility (custom policies, REST APIs) to enforce consent and data control.

- Implement self-service user portals for data access and deletion.

- Minimize data collection and disclose usage clearly.

- Use Application Insights for logging and monitoring.

- Create an internal compliance checklist for new features.

- Work with your legal team to ensure policies and flows meet local and international standards.

Summary

Compliance is not a one-time task, but an ongoing responsibility. Azure AD B2C provides the flexibility and security required to meet the demands of modern data privacy regulations. When configured thoughtfully, it becomes a powerful ally in your compliance strategy, ensuring that user trust is maintained and regulatory risks are minimized.

In the next section, we'll explore real-world deployment stories and lessons learned from enterprise-scale Azure AD B2C implementations.

Lessons Learned from Enterprise Deployments

Enterprise-scale deployments of Azure AD B2C reveal both the power and the complexity of leveraging a flexible identity solution in real-world scenarios. Organizations deploying B2C at scale have to navigate challenges related to scalability, customization, security, governance, integration, and user experience — all while maintaining regulatory compliance and delivering performance.

This section distills lessons learned from enterprise Azure AD B2C implementations across industries such as finance, healthcare, education, and retail. The focus is on patterns that work, common pitfalls, performance tuning, infrastructure strategies, and architectural decisions proven in production environments.

Strategic Planning and Governance

Before deploying Azure AD B2C in a large enterprise, establish a clear governance model:

1. Tenant Ownership and Role Delegation

Avoid the trap of having a single administrator or department manage everything. Use **Role-Based Access Control (RBAC)** to segment duties:

- **Global Admins**: Azure subscription and billing.

- **B2C Admins**: Manage user flows and policies.

- **Developers**: Application registration and integration.

- **Security Auditors**: Access to logs and audit trails.

```
// Sample Azure role assignment

{

  "roleDefinitionId":
"/providers/Microsoft.Authorization/roleDefinitions/...",

  "principalId": "user-object-id",

  "scope":
"/subscriptions/.../resourceGroups/.../providers/Microsoft.AzureActi
veDirectory/b2cDirectories/..."

}
```

2. Naming Conventions

Use consistent naming conventions for:

- Policies   (B2C_1A_SignUpSignIn_TenantX)

- Applications   (MyApp-Web-Prod,   MyApp-API-Test)

- API   scopes   (https://myapp.com/api/read)

This makes automation, scripting, and CI/CD pipelines more reliable.

Custom Policies: Complexity and Power

Many enterprises move from built-in user flows to **custom policies** (Identity Experience Framework) to gain advanced control over identity journeys. However, this shift introduces complexity.

Lessons:

- **Modularize your policies**: Separate base policies from extensions (e.g., TrustFrameworkBase.xml,   TrustFrameworkExtensions.xml).

- **Version control policies** in Git to enable rollback and collaboration.

- **Validate locally** using Run now in the Azure portal or a script to simulate journeys.

- **Use Application Insights** to debug execution paths and rule evaluations.

Example Directory Structure

```
/policies

  /base

    TrustFrameworkBase.xml

  /extensions

    TrustFrameworkExtensions.xml

  /custom

    SignUpOrSignIn.xml

    ProfileEdit.xml
```

REST API Integration

RESTful API claims providers are frequently used to:

- Validate user input (e.g., verify phone numbers, promo codes)
- Enrich tokens with external data (e.g., user roles, preferences)
- Call fraud detection systems

Tips:

- Make APIs idempotent and fast (under 300ms ideal).
- Include correlation IDs for troubleshooting.
- Use App Service or Azure Functions with autoscale enabled.

Sample REST Provider

```
<TechnicalProfile Id="REST-GetRoles">

  <DisplayName>Get User Roles</DisplayName>

  <Protocol                                    Name="Proprietary"
Handler="Web.TPEngine.Providers.RestfulProvider" />

  <Metadata>

    <Item Key="ServiceUrl">https://myapi.com/identity/roles</Item>

    <Item Key="AuthenticationType">None</Item>

    <Item Key="SendClaimsIn">Body</Item>

  </Metadata>

  <InputClaims>

    <InputClaim ClaimTypeReferenceId="email" />

  </InputClaims>

  <OutputClaims>

    <OutputClaim ClaimTypeReferenceId="role" />
```

```
    </OutputClaims>

</TechnicalProfile>
```

Scalability and Performance Tuning

Enterprises often experience high traffic volumes during product launches or marketing campaigns. Azure AD B2C handles this well when planned correctly.

Recommendations:

- **Custom Domains**: Use `login.brand.com` to enhance trust and minimize redirect issues.

- **Token lifetimes**: Configure via Azure CLI to balance security and user experience.

- **Session behavior**: Adjust `Keep me signed in` and SSO lifetimes to reduce reauthentication.

CLI Command for Token Lifetime

```
az ad b2c policy set-token-lifetime \

  --name B2C_1A_SignIn \

  --access-token-lifetime PT1H \

  --id-token-lifetime PT1H
```

Application Insights can monitor average execution time for each orchestration step to spot bottlenecks.

Branding and UX Challenges

In enterprise settings with multiple brands or subsidiaries, customizing the experience dynamically is essential.

Lessons:

- Store brand themes in a database or CMS.

- Pass `ui_locales` or query string parameters to user flows to load branding dynamically.

- Use `JavaScript` in the policy UI to adjust logos, colors, field visibility.

Branding Logic Example

```
const tenantBrand = localStorage.getItem("brand");

if (tenantBrand === "Contoso") {

  document.getElementById("logo").src = "/logos/contoso.png";

  document.body.style.backgroundColor = "#003366";

}
```

Testing and Staging Environments

Always maintain separate environments:

- **Dev**: Developer testing with low risk.

- **Test**: Used by QA with production-like data.

- **Prod**: Live user environment.

Best Practices:

- Use separate B2C tenants or prefix policies with `DEV_`, `TEST_`, `PROD_`.

- Mirror policy versions across environments using Git and CI/CD.

- Automate deployment of policies using PowerShell or Azure DevOps pipelines.

Example Deployment Script

```
Import-AzureADPolicy    -TenantId    $tenantId    -PolicyPath
".\policies\SignUpOrSignIn.xml"
```

Integration with Microsoft 365 and Enterprise Identity

Large enterprises often require sign-in via both:

- B2C local/social accounts (customers)

- Azure AD enterprise accounts (partners, B2B users)

Configure **identity providers** in custom policies and route dynamically based on email domain.

```
<ClaimsTransformation                               Id="EmailDomainCheck"
TransformationMethod="AssertBooleanClaimIsEqualToValue">

  <InputClaims>

    <InputClaim ClaimTypeReferenceId="email_domain" />

  </InputClaims>

  <InputParameters>

    <InputParameter Id="value" DataType="string" Value="contoso.com"
/>

  </InputParameters>

</ClaimsTransformation>
```

This enables routing corporate domains to Azure AD and others to B2C login.

Security and Threat Mitigation

Security at scale includes:

- **MFA policies**: Enforced based on risk, geo, or transaction type.

- **IP filtering**: Limit access to sensitive APIs via WAF or NSGs.

- **Audit logs**: Integrated with SIEM for alerting and compliance.

Use **Conditional Access** in combination with B2C sign-in to apply risk-based controls.

Conditional MFA Example

```
<OrchestrationStep Order="2" Type="ClaimsExchange">

  <ClaimsExchanges>

    <ClaimsExchange                                    Id="MFA"
TechnicalProfileReferenceId="PhoneFactor-InputOrVerify" />

  </ClaimsExchanges>

</OrchestrationStep>
```

Pair this with device fingerprinting or IP reputation services for stronger defense.

Logging and Supportability

At enterprise scale, you'll need structured telemetry:

- **Correlate user journey IDs** with backend logs.
- **Track policy execution times** per request.
- **Alert on errors** from REST API connectors.

Use **App Insights custom events**:

```
appInsights.trackEvent({

  name: "SignInStart",

  properties: {

    correlationId: "abc-123",

    policy: "B2C_1A_SignIn"

  }

});
```

Store logs with retention policies that align with data protection standards and internal audits.

Organizational Change Management

Deploying Azure AD B2C is as much an organizational shift as it is a technical one.

Tips:

- **Train product teams** to understand identity lifecycle management.
- **Involve compliance teams** early for approval on flows and consent.
- **Educate customer support** on password resets, MFA issues, and sign-in patterns.

Prepare internal documentation and offer support runbooks. Consider providing a branded admin portal for non-technical team members to invite users or view logs.

Summary

Enterprise deployments of Azure AD B2C succeed when there is alignment across architecture, governance, security, and operations. The key lessons include:

- Modularizing and versioning policies from the start
- Automating everything (policy uploads, branding updates, telemetry)
- Using REST APIs to enhance tokens with app-specific claims
- Prioritizing performance monitoring and user experience
- Treating identity as a product, not just a technical necessity

When executed well, Azure AD B2C scales to support millions of users, thousands of brands, and dozens of countries — while enabling rich customization, strict security, and regulatory compliance.

Next, the appendices provide code samples, glossary terms, and additional resources to support your Azure AD B2C journey.

Chapter 11: Appendices

Glossary of Terms

Understanding Azure AD B2C and identity management requires familiarity with a number of technical terms and concepts. This glossary provides clear definitions of the most commonly encountered terms in this field, helping to demystify jargon and establish a shared understanding. Whether you're a developer, architect, or IT admin, this section can serve as a quick reference throughout your Azure AD B2C journey.

Access Token

A token issued by Azure AD B2C that grants an application permission to access a specific resource (such as an API). Access tokens are short-lived and contain claims used by the resource server to authorize requests.

Application Registration

The process of registering an app with Azure AD B2C, allowing it to use identity features such as authentication and token acquisition. Each application receives a unique client ID and optionally a client secret.

Azure AD B2C (Azure Active Directory Business to Consumer)

A cloud-based identity and access management solution tailored for consumer-facing applications. Azure AD B2C enables customers to sign up, sign in, and manage profiles securely across multiple channels.

Bearer Token

A security token provided by Azure AD B2C (usually an access token) that must be included in HTTP requests to protected APIs. The token proves that the user is authenticated and authorized.

Claims

Assertions about the user, such as name, email, or custom attributes, that are included in tokens. Claims are crucial for identity transformation, access control, and personalization in apps.

Client ID

A unique identifier assigned to an application when it's registered with Azure AD B2C. It is used to identify the app when requesting tokens.

Client Secret

A password-like credential used by confidential apps to authenticate to Azure AD B2C during token acquisition. It must be stored securely and not exposed in public-facing code.

Custom Policies (Identity Experience Framework)

Custom XML-based policies that define complex user journeys and integrations in Azure AD B2C. They offer granular control over authentication and authorization processes beyond built-in user flows.

Directory

A container in Azure AD that holds users, groups, apps, and other resources. Each B2C tenant is essentially an Azure AD directory configured for external identities.

Federation

A trust relationship established between Azure AD B2C and external identity providers (e.g., Google, Facebook, custom OpenID Connect providers). Federation allows users to authenticate using existing credentials.

ID Token

A JSON Web Token (JWT) issued by Azure AD B2C that contains user profile information (claims). It is primarily used by client apps to personalize the UI and confirm authentication.

Identity Provider (IdP)

A service that authenticates users and issues tokens. Azure AD B2C supports built-in local identity providers as well as third-party providers like Facebook, Google, and enterprise IdPs via SAML/OpenID Connect.

JWT (JSON Web Token)

An open standard (RFC 7519) format for securely transmitting information between parties. Azure AD B2C uses JWTs for access and ID tokens, with a header, payload, and signature.

Example of a decoded JWT payload:

```
{

  "name": "John Doe",

  "email": "john.doe@example.com",

  "iss": "https://yourtenant.b2clogin.com/",

  "aud": "your-client-id",

  "exp": 1710177335

}
```

Local Account

An identity that is created and stored natively within Azure AD B2C. Users can sign up with an email address or username and a password directly managed by the B2C tenant.

Multifactor Authentication (MFA)

A security process requiring two or more forms of verification. Azure AD B2C supports MFA via SMS and authenticator apps for improved account protection.

OpenID Connect (OIDC)

An authentication protocol based on OAuth 2.0. Azure AD B2C uses OIDC to integrate with apps and identity providers, supporting secure sign-in and token issuance.

Policy (User Flow)

A predefined set of steps for handling user sign-up, sign-in, profile editing, or password reset in Azure AD B2C. Built-in user flows are easy to configure via the Azure portal.

Refresh Token

A long-lived token used to obtain new access tokens after the previous ones expire. It allows users to stay signed in without re-entering credentials.

Reply URL / Redirect URI

The endpoint in your application to which Azure AD B2C sends responses after authentication. It must match the URI registered in the B2C application configuration.

RESTful API Connector

A mechanism in Azure AD B2C to call external APIs during a user journey (e.g., to validate user data or enrich claims). They are typically invoked in custom policies.

Example XML snippet:

```
<TechnicalProfile Id="REST-GetUserDetails">

  <DisplayName>Call REST API</DisplayName>

  <Protocol Name="Proprietary" />

  <Metadata>

    <Item
Key="ServiceUrl">https://api.example.com/userdetails</Item>

    <Item Key="AuthenticationType">None</Item>
```

```
    <Item Key="SendClaimsIn">Body</Item>

  </Metadata>

</TechnicalProfile>
```

Relying Party (RP)

An application or service that relies on Azure AD B2C for authentication. The RP receives tokens from B2C and uses them to authorize users.

SAML (Security Assertion Markup Language)

An XML-based standard for exchanging authentication and authorization data. Azure AD B2C supports federation with enterprise IdPs via SAML 2.0.

Scopes

Defined permissions that an application can request from users. For example, an app might request `openid`, `profile`, and `email` scopes to access corresponding claims in the token.

Session Token

A token that represents the session state between the user and Azure AD B2C. Session tokens can be configured for duration and persistence to control sign-in behavior.

Sign-In Policy

A user flow or custom policy designed specifically for authenticating users. It can include social login, local account login, and MFA requirements.

Sign-Up Policy

A user journey for registering new users in Azure AD B2C. It often includes attributes collection, terms of service acceptance, and email verification.

Single Sign-On (SSO)

A user authentication process that allows access to multiple applications with one set of credentials. Azure AD B2C supports SSO within the same tenant and across apps sharing a session.

Tenant

A dedicated instance of Azure AD B2C that houses all identity and policy configurations for a given organization or solution.

Token Endpoint

A URL exposed by Azure AD B2C to issue and refresh tokens. It is used in OAuth 2.0 flows and typically looks like:

```
https://<tenant-name>.b2clogin.com/<tenant-
id>/oauth2/v2.0/token?p=<policy-name>
```

Token Lifetimes

The duration for which tokens are valid before expiring. These settings can be customized using Azure AD B2C policy configurations.

User Attributes

Properties collected from or about the user, such as display name, job title, or custom metadata. These attributes are stored in the directory and can be mapped to claims in policies.

User Journey

The complete process a user goes through during an interaction, including sign-up, sign-in, MFA, and claims transformation. Defined using either user flows or custom policies.

This glossary should remain open while working through the remainder of the book, as many of these terms will continue to appear in configuration examples, code, and best practices discussions. For quick lookups and deeper understanding, this section is designed to grow with your familiarity and usage of Azure AD B2C.

Resources for Further Learning

This section offers a comprehensive and structured list of valuable resources, tools, and platforms that will deepen your understanding of Azure AD B2C and its ecosystem. Whether you're a beginner aiming to build your first integration or an enterprise architect creating advanced identity experiences, these materials will serve as long-term companions on your development journey.

Microsoft Official Documentation

The official Microsoft Azure AD B2C documentation is the most authoritative source of knowledge. It is continuously updated with new features, best practices, API references, and sample walkthroughs. Key sections include:

- **Overview   and   Concepts**
  https://learn.microsoft.com/en-us/azure/active-directory-b2c/overview

- **Quickstarts**
  Step-by-step tutorials to build and integrate sign-up/sign-in flows with popular platforms like ASP.NET, React, Angular, and mobile apps.
  https://learn.microsoft.com/en-us/azure/active-directory-b2c/quickstarts-overview

- **Custom   Policy   Documentation**
  The most detailed and in-depth explanations on the Identity Experience Framework, schema structure, claims transformation, REST API orchestration, and more.
  https://learn.microsoft.com/en-us/azure/active-directory-b2c/custom-policy-overview

- **User   Flow   Configuration**
  Understand how to configure pre-built user flows without writing XML, including email signup, password reset, and profile editing.
  https://learn.microsoft.com/en-us/azure/active-directory-b2c/user-flow-overview

- **Token   Reference   and   Claims   Mapping**
  Learn how tokens are structured and how to map user attributes to specific claims.
  https://learn.microsoft.com/en-us/azure/active-directory-b2c/tokens-overview

GitHub Repositories

GitHub is a goldmine of open-source samples and community-driven tools for Azure AD B2C.

- **Azure   Samples   Repository**
  Microsoft's official Azure AD B2C samples repository includes code in multiple languages, examples of RESTful API integration, user journey samples, and more. https://github.com/Azure-Samples

  Notable   sub-repositories:

    o   active-directory-b2c-custom-policy-starterpack

    o   active-directory-b2c-advanced-policies

    o   active-directory-b2c-identityprovider-facebook

- **Community   Tools**
  Repositories from MVPs and other identity experts offer niche tools like XML schema validators,   policy   testers,   and   emulators   for   local   debugging.

Microsoft Learn and Training Paths

Microsoft Learn provides structured learning paths with interactive exercises and sandbox environments:

- **Identity   Management   Learning   Path**
  https://learn.microsoft.com/en-us/training/paths/secure-apps-with-identity/

- **Manage   External   Identities**
  Focused   on   managing   B2C   and   B2B   identities   in   Azure. https://learn.microsoft.com/en-us/training/modules/manage-external-identities-azure-ad/

- **Free   Labs   with   Sandbox   Environments**
  These give you temporary Azure subscriptions to test out Azure AD B2C configurations   without   needing   a   personal   or   organizational   tenant. https://learn.microsoft.com/en-us/training/azure/

Books and eBooks

A growing number of books have been published that go beyond documentation and offer curated guidance. Some of the best titles include:

- **"Modern Authentication with Azure Active Directory for Web Applications"** by **Vittorio** **Bertocci**
  While it focuses on Azure AD, it lays down the foundational knowledge that applies to B2C.

- **"Implementing Azure Solutions"** by **Florian Klaffenbach et al.**
  Includes a section on Azure AD B2C and its implementation in modern cloud architecture.

- **Microsoft Press eBooks**
  These are free and often updated with each major Azure milestone. Look out for identity-related ones:
  https://learn.microsoft.com/en-us/ebooks/

Video Courses and YouTube Channels

- **Microsoft Developer YouTube Channel**
  This channel features product demos, new release walk-throughs, and live webinars covering Azure identity topics.
  https://www.youtube.com/c/MicrosoftDeveloper

- **John Savill's Technical Training**
  Offers deep-dive tutorials, including step-by-step setup for Azure AD B2C tenants and advanced policy design.
  https://www.youtube.com/c/JohnSavillTechnicalTraining

- **Pluralsight Courses**
  In-depth video courses on identity management, Azure AD, and security from industry experts. Topics include secure authentication flows, token management, and Azure CLI integration.

Community Blogs and Technical Articles

- **Auth0 vs Azure AD B2C**
  Comparisons of popular identity platforms. Useful if you're deciding on vendor-neutral architecture.
  Examples:

- ○ Auth0   Blog

- ○ Medium   articles   by   identity   professionals

- ○ Dev.to   articles   tagged   with   #azureb2c

- **Microsoft**   **Tech**   **Community**   **Blog**
  Frequently features real-world Azure AD B2C case studies and new feature releases.
  https://techcommunity.microsoft.com/t5/azure-active-directory-identity/bg-p/Azure-Active-Directory-Identity

- **Stack**   **Overflow**
  The `azure-ad-b2c` tag is actively monitored by both Microsoft engineers and the developer   community.
  https://stackoverflow.com/questions/tagged/azure-ad-b2c

Sample Projects and Templates

These projects are ideal for jumpstarting development or validating architecture patterns.

React SPA + Azure AD B2C Authentication

- Uses   MSAL.js

- Supports   silent   token   renewal   and   redirect   flow

- Backend   optional

```
npx create-react-app my-b2c-app

cd my-b2c-app

npm install @azure/msal-browser @azure/msal-react
```

```
import { PublicClientApplication } from "@azure/msal-browser";


const msalConfig = {
```

```
auth: {

    clientId: "your-client-id",

    authority:
"https://yourtenant.b2clogin.com/yourtenant.onmicrosoft.com/B2C_1_si
gnupsignin",

    redirectUri: "http://localhost:3000"

}

};
```

```
const msalInstance = new PublicClientApplication(msalConfig);
```

ASP.NET Core Web API + Azure AD B2C Protection

- Token   validation   using   Microsoft.Identity.Web

- Enforces   scopes   for   granular   access

```
services.AddAuthentication(JwtBearerDefaults.AuthenticationScheme)
```

```
.AddMicrosoftIdentityWebApi(Configuration.GetSection("AzureAdB2C"));
```

```
"AzureAdB2C": {

  "Instance": "https://yourtenant.b2clogin.com/",

  "ClientId": "api-client-id",

  "Domain": "yourtenant.onmicrosoft.com",

  "SignUpSignInPolicyId": "B2C_1_signupsignin"
```

}

Developer Tools and SDKs

- **MSAL** **Libraries**
  SDKs available for .NET, JavaScript, Python, iOS, Android, and more
  https://learn.microsoft.com/en-us/azure/active-directory/develop/msal-overview

Azure **CLI** **and** **PowerShell**
Ideal for scripting tenant management, app registration, and policy deployment
Examples:

bash

```
az login

az ad b2c directory create --display-name "My B2C Tenant"
```

-
- **Postman** **Collections**
  Helpful for testing RESTful API connectors or token acquisition

    - Custom environments for tenant variables

    - Sample workflows for login and refresh

Podcasts and Industry Conversations

- **Azure** **Friday** **(Microsoft)**
  Often features identity architects discussing real implementations
  https://azure.microsoft.com/en-us/shows/azure-friday/

- **Identity,** **Unlocked** **(by** **Auth0)**
  In-depth look into identity standards like OpenID Connect, JWT, SAML, and OAuth
  from protocol designers and contributors.

Forums and Support Channels

- **Microsoft** **Q&A**
  Community-powered with moderation from Microsoft identity team
  https://learn.microsoft.com/en-us/answers/topics/azure-ad-b2c.html

- **Azure** **Feedback** **Portal**
  Suggest new features, upvote existing requests, and follow roadmap items
  https://feedback.azure.com/d365community/forum/0f0c54b3-22f6-ec11-b6e6-000d3a4f07b8

- **Slack** **and** **Discord** **Developer** **Communities**
  While not officially supported, many developers find faster troubleshooting in Slack workspaces and Discord channels focused on Azure and identity.

By combining official documentation, structured courses, real-world samples, and active community involvement, you'll gain a holistic understanding of Azure AD B2C. Bookmark this section and revisit it regularly to explore new releases, patterns, and productivity tools.

Sample Projects and Code Snippets

This section presents a wide collection of sample projects and code snippets designed to help you implement Azure AD B2C in various application types. These practical examples range from beginner-friendly templates to advanced integrations involving REST APIs, custom policies, and multi-platform support. Each sample is curated to demonstrate a specific use case or design pattern, and many are ready to clone, configure, and deploy.

Single Page Applications (React, Angular, Vue)

Single-page applications (SPAs) are a common use case for Azure AD B2C. These apps rely heavily on token-based authentication and require tight integration with the Microsoft Authentication Library (MSAL).

React + MSAL.js

React apps benefit from the `@azure/msal-react` wrapper for cleaner hooks and components.

Installation:

```
npm install @azure/msal-browser @azure/msal-react
```

Configuration:

```ts
// src/authConfig.ts
export const msalConfig = {
  auth: {
    clientId: "your-client-id",
    authority:
"https://yourtenant.b2clogin.com/yourtenant.onmicrosoft.com/B2C_1_signupsignin",
    redirectUri: "http://localhost:3000"
  }
};
```

App Initialization:

```tsx
// src/index.tsx
import { PublicClientApplication } from "@azure/msal-browser";
import { MsalProvider } from "@azure/msal-react";
import { msalConfig } from "./authConfig";


const msalInstance = new PublicClientApplication(msalConfig);


ReactDOM.render(
  <MsalProvider instance={msalInstance}>
    <App />
  </MsalProvider>,
```

```
  document.getElementById("root")

);
```

Using the Hook:

```
import { useMsal } from "@azure/msal-react";


const SignInButton = () => {

  const { instance } = useMsal();

  return  <button  onClick={()  =>  instance.loginRedirect()}>Sign
In</button>;

};
```

Backend APIs (Node.js, ASP.NET Core)

To protect APIs using Azure AD B2C, configure token validation middleware.

ASP.NET Core with Microsoft.Identity.Web

Startup.cs:

```
services.AddAuthentication(JwtBearerDefaults.AuthenticationScheme)

    .AddMicrosoftIdentityWebApi(Configuration, "AzureAdB2C");
```

appsettings.json:

```
"AzureAdB2C": {

  "Instance": "https://yourtenant.b2clogin.com/",
```

```
"ClientId": "api-client-id",

"Domain": "yourtenant.onmicrosoft.com",

"SignUpSignInPolicyId": "B2C_1_signupsignin"

}
```

Controller Sample:

```
[Authorize]

[ApiController]

[Route("[controller]")]

public class ProfileController : ControllerBase

{

    [HttpGet]

    public IActionResult Get() => Ok(new { Message = "Authenticated user" });

}
```

Mobile Apps (React Native, Xamarin, Flutter)

Azure AD B2C supports mobile apps through MSAL libraries tailored for each platform.

React Native + Expo (with Web Redirect)

Install Dependencies:

```
npx expo install expo-auth-session

npm install @azure/msal-browser
```

Authentication Flow:

```
import * as AuthSession from "expo-auth-session";


const discovery = {

  authorizationEndpoint:
"https://yourtenant.b2clogin.com/yourtenant.onmicrosoft.com/B2C_1_si
gnupsignin/oauth2/v2.0/authorize",

  tokenEndpoint:
"https://yourtenant.b2clogin.com/yourtenant.onmicrosoft.com/B2C_1_si
gnupsignin/oauth2/v2.0/token"

};


const useAzureAuth = async () => {

  const   redirectUri   =   AuthSession.makeRedirectUri({   native:
"yourapp://" });

  const result = await AuthSession.startAsync({

    authUrl:      `${discovery.authorizationEndpoint}?client_id=your-
client-
id&response_type=token&redirect_uri=${encodeURIComponent(redirectUri
)}&scope=openid profile`

  });


  if (result.type === "success") {

    const accessToken = result.params.access_token;

    // Store and use token

  }
```

```
};
```

Custom Policy Samples

Using Identity Experience Framework (IEF), custom policies allow extreme flexibility. Here are some reusable snippets.

Collecting a Custom Attribute

In `TrustFrameworkExtensions.xml`:

```
<ClaimType Id="extension_favoriteColor">

  <DisplayName>Favorite Color</DisplayName>

  <DataType>string</DataType>

  <DefaultPartnerClaimTypes>

    <Protocol Name="OAuth2" PartnerClaimType="favorite_color" />

  </DefaultPartnerClaimTypes>

  <UserHelpText>Enter your favorite color</UserHelpText>

</ClaimType>
```

Add this to your `SelfAsserted-LocalAccountSignin-Email` technical profile input claims.

```
<InputClaim ClaimTypeReferenceId="extension_favoriteColor" />
```

RESTful API Integration in Custom Policies

You can call external services during a user journey. This is useful for fraud checks, data enrichment, or custom validation.

Example: Checking User Email in External DB

```
<TechnicalProfile Id="REST-CheckEmail">

  <DisplayName>Verify Email Against External DB</DisplayName>

  <Protocol Name="Proprietary" />

  <Metadata>

    <Item Key="ServiceUrl">https://api.example.com/checkemail</Item>

    <Item Key="SendClaimsIn">Body</Item>

  </Metadata>

  <InputClaims>

    <InputClaim ClaimTypeReferenceId="email" />

  </InputClaims>

  <OutputClaims>

    <OutputClaim ClaimTypeReferenceId="emailExists" />

  </OutputClaims>

</TechnicalProfile>
```

Multi-Tenant SaaS App Sample

This project demonstrates dynamic policy resolution and branding per tenant using custom policies.

High-Level Architecture:

- App   registration   allows   multi-tenant   access

- Domain lookup determines policy and branding
- Policies reference tenant-specific content definitions

Sample ClaimsTransformation:

```xml
<ClaimsTransformation Id="ResolveTenantPolicy" TransformationMethod="FormatString">
  <InputClaims>
    <InputClaim ClaimTypeReferenceId="domain" TransformationClaimType="inputClaim1" />
  </InputClaims>
  <InputParameters>
    <InputParameter Id="stringFormat" DataType="string" Value="B2C_1A_Tenant_{0}_Policy" />
  </InputParameters>
  <OutputClaims>
    <OutputClaim ClaimTypeReferenceId="resolvedPolicy" TransformationClaimType="outputClaim" />
  </OutputClaims>
</ClaimsTransformation>
```

Passwordless Authentication Sample

Implementing email-based one-time codes via built-in user flows or custom policies.

Built-In Approach:

1. Create a user flow of type "Sign up and sign in".

2. Choose "Email with OTP (preview)" as the identity provider.

3. Enable MFA if needed.

Custom Policy Snippet (for email code):

```xml
<TechnicalProfile Id="Email-OTP">

  <DisplayName>Email One Time Passcode</DisplayName>

  <Protocol Name="Proprietary" />

  <Metadata>

    <Item Key="ContentDefinitionReferenceId">api.emailotp</Item>

    <Item Key="SendOtp">true</Item>

  </Metadata>

  <InputClaims>

    <InputClaim ClaimTypeReferenceId="email" />

  </InputClaims>

</TechnicalProfile>
```

Automated CI/CD Deployment with GitHub Actions

You can automate policy validation and publishing using GitHub workflows.

Sample Workflow:

```yaml
name: Deploy B2C Policies


on:
```

```
  push:

    branches: [main]


jobs:

  deploy:

    runs-on: ubuntu-latest

    steps:

      - name: Checkout

        uses: actions/checkout@v3


      - name: Upload Custom Policies

        run: |

          az login --service-principal -u ${{ secrets.CLIENT_ID }} -p ${{ secrets.CLIENT_SECRET }} --tenant ${{ secrets.TENANT_ID }}

          az rest --method PUT \

            --uri https://graph.microsoft.com/beta/trustFramework/policies/B2C_1A_signup_signin \

            --body @./policies/TrustFrameworkPolicy.xml \

            --headers "Content-Type=application/xml"
```

Offline Token Validation for APIs

When using a backend, validating JWTs offline can improve performance.

Node.js Sample with jsonwebtoken:

```
const jwt = require('jsonwebtoken');


const decoded = jwt.verify(token, publicKey, {

  audience: "your-client-id",

  issuer:
"https://yourtenant.b2clogin.com/yourtenant.onmicrosoft.com/v2.0/"

});
```

This comprehensive set of sample projects and code snippets can be used as templates or extended into production systems. Clone, test, and modify them to meet your needs. Always follow best practices regarding token storage, secure API access, and policy validation before going live.

API Reference Guide

This section provides a detailed reference for working with the core APIs in Azure AD B2C. Azure AD B2C is built on top of Azure Active Directory and follows industry standards like OAuth 2.0 and OpenID Connect. As a result, developers interact primarily with endpoints for token acquisition, user authentication, user management, and directory access. This guide will walk through both high-level and low-level API endpoints, their parameters, and practical examples for integrating them into applications.

Authorization and Token Endpoints

Azure AD B2C uses standard OAuth 2.0 endpoints with B2C-specific formatting. These endpoints are policy-driven, meaning the policy name must be included in the URL.

Token Endpoint

Format:

```
POST                      https://<tenant-name>.b2clogin.com/<tenant-
name>.onmicrosoft.com/<policy-name>/oauth2/v2.0/token
```

Headers:

```
Content-Type: application/x-www-form-urlencoded
```

Body Parameters:

- `client_id`: Your app's client ID
- `scope`: Must include `openid` plus any API scopes
- `grant_type`: One of `authorization_code`, `refresh_token`, or `client_credentials`
- `code`: (if using `authorization_code`) the code received after sign-in
- `redirect_uri`: Same redirect URI used during sign-in
- `client_secret`: (if using confidential clients)

Example Request (Authorization Code Flow):

```
curl -X POST
https://yourtenant.b2clogin.com/yourtenant.onmicrosoft.com/B2C_1_sig
nupsignin/oauth2/v2.0/token \

-H "Content-Type: application/x-www-form-urlencoded" \

-d
"grant_type=authorization_code&client_id=YOUR_CLIENT_ID&code=YOUR_CO
DE&redirect_uri=http://localhost:3000&scope=openid%20offline_access&
client_secret=YOUR_SECRET"
```

Response:

```
{
  "access_token": "eyJ...",
```

```
"id_token": "eyJ...",

"refresh_token": "eyJ...",

"expires_in": 3600,

"token_type": "Bearer"

}
```

OpenID Connect Metadata

Metadata discovery is essential for clients using OpenID Connect. Azure AD B2C provides a metadata document for each policy.

URL Format:

```
https://<tenant-name>.b2clogin.com/<tenant-
name>.onmicrosoft.com/<policy-name>/v2.0/.well-known/openid-
configuration
```

Example:

```
https://yourtenant.b2clogin.com/yourtenant.onmicrosoft.com/B2C_1_sig
nupsignin/v2.0/.well-known/openid-configuration
```

This endpoint returns a JSON object describing token endpoints, authorization endpoints, supported claims, signing keys, and more.

User Info Endpoint

After obtaining an access token, you can use the user info endpoint to retrieve user profile details.

Endpoint:

```
GET                      https://<tenant-name>.b2clogin.com/<tenant-
name>.onmicrosoft.com/<policy-name>/openid/v2.0/userinfo
```

Headers:

```
Authorization: Bearer <access_token>
```

Response Example:

```
{

  "sub": "248289761001",

  "name": "Jane Doe",

  "email": "janedoe@example.com"

}
```

Note: This endpoint is limited and may only return standard OpenID Connect claims.

Microsoft Graph API

While Azure AD B2C doesn't expose its own unique API for managing users, it uses Microsoft Graph with some restrictions and extensions. The Microsoft Graph API allows you to programmatically manage users, groups, and directory objects.

Graph API Base URL:

```
https://graph.microsoft.com/v1.0/
```

Create a B2C User:

```
POST https://graph.microsoft.com/v1.0/users

Content-Type: application/json

Authorization: Bearer <admin_token>
```

Request Body:

```json
{

  "accountEnabled": true,

  "displayName": "John Smith",

  "mailNickname": "johnsmith",

  "userPrincipalName": "johnsmith@yourtenant.onmicrosoft.com",

  "passwordProfile": {

    "forceChangePasswordNextSignIn": false,

    "password": "ComplexP@ssword!"

  },

  "identities": [

    {

      "signInType": "emailAddress",

      "issuer": "yourtenant.onmicrosoft.com",

      "issuerAssignedId": "johnsmith@example.com"

    }

  ]

}
```

Refresh Tokens

Refresh tokens allow clients to obtain new access tokens without requiring the user to sign in again.

Token Request:

```
curl                              -X                          POST
https://yourtenant.b2clogin.com/yourtenant.onmicrosoft.com/B2C_1_sig
nupsignin/oauth2/v2.0/token \

-H "Content-Type: application/x-www-form-urlencoded" \

-d
"grant_type=refresh_token&client_id=YOUR_CLIENT_ID&refresh_token=YOU
R_REFRESH_TOKEN&redirect_uri=http://localhost:3000&scope=openid%20of
fline_access&client_secret=YOUR_SECRET"
```

Session Management APIs

Azure AD B2C doesn't expose formal session management APIs but includes session settings in policies:

- `SingleSignOnScope`

- `SessionExpiryInSeconds`

- `KeepAliveInSeconds`

These are defined within the `RelyingParty` or `OrchestrationStep`.

Example Snippet:

```
<SessionExpiryType>Rolling</SessionExpiryType>

<SessionExpiryInSeconds>3600</SessionExpiryInSeconds>
```

```
<KeepAliveInSeconds>900</KeepAliveInSeconds>
```

These settings help control cookie expiration and refresh behavior.

JWKs and Token Validation

Tokens are signed using public keys, which are rotated periodically. Apps should use the JWKs endpoint to validate the token signature.

JWKS Endpoint:

```
https://<tenant-name>.b2clogin.com/<tenant-
name>.onmicrosoft.com/<policy-name>/discovery/v2.0/keys
```

Sample Response:

```
{
  "keys": [
    {
      "kty": "RSA",
      "use": "sig",
      "kid": "X5xk5ljs29R...",
      "e": "AQAB",
      "n": "4xN7Z-8..."
    }
  ]
}
```

Use libraries like `jsonwebtoken`, `Microsoft.IdentityModel.Tokens`, or `nimbus-jose-jwt` to validate signatures based on this data.

B2C Extensions App and Custom Attributes

Azure AD B2C creates an **extensions app** in the background, which allows storing custom user attributes.

Example:

A custom attribute called `extension_favoriteColor` would be added as:

```
{

  "extension_favoriteColor": "Blue"

}
```

When using Graph, custom attributes must use their full schema extension format.

Sample Patch:

```
PATCH https://graph.microsoft.com/v1.0/users/{user-id}

Authorization: Bearer <admin_token>

Content-Type: application/json
```

Body:

```
{

  "extension_<appId>_favoriteColor": "Green"

}
```

Using Application Insights with B2C

Although not a direct API, B2C supports outputting logs to Application Insights for diagnostics.

Enable via Custom Policy:

```
<InstrumentationKey>Your_Instrumentation_Key</InstrumentationKey>
```

Query Logs in Kusto:

```
customEvents
| where name == "OrchestrationStepCompleted"
| project timestamp, name, customDimensions
```

Application Insights logs can expose claim values, execution steps, REST API responses, and errors during sign-up/sign-in flows.

Revoking Tokens and Logouts

Azure AD B2C doesn't currently support programmatic token revocation. However, you can perform front-channel logout using:

Logout URL:

```
https://<tenant-name>.b2clogin.com/<tenant-
name>.onmicrosoft.com/<policy-name>/oauth2/v2.0/logout?p=<policy-
name>&post_logout_redirect_uri=https://yourapp.com
```

Calling this URL clears the user's session at the Azure AD B2C level and redirects to the provided URI.

Best Practices When Using APIs

- **Use HTTPS only** for all token and Graph API requests.

- **Do not store tokens in localStorage** in browser apps; prefer sessionStorage or secure memory.

- **Refresh tokens securely** and store them only in server-side apps or using secure device storage.

- **Scope tokens tightly** to only required permissions to reduce blast radius in case of leaks.

- **Validate all incoming tokens** against metadata and JWKs.

- **Avoid hardcoding secrets** — use environment variables or managed identity where applicable.

This API reference guide empowers developers to leverage Azure AD B2C's underlying standards and endpoints to build secure, scalable identity experiences. Keep this section handy for debugging flows, integrating custom clients, or automating tenant operations.

Frequently Asked Questions

This section compiles the most frequently asked questions about Azure AD B2C, covering everything from setup and configuration to security, custom policies, application integration, and troubleshooting. These questions have been sourced from real-world implementations, developer forums, enterprise rollouts, and feedback from the Microsoft identity community.

How is Azure AD B2C different from Azure AD?

Azure AD is designed for managing internal users within an organization—employees, contractors, and partners. It supports B2B collaboration, device management, and enterprise applications like Microsoft 365.

Azure AD B2C, on the other hand, is purpose-built for external or consumer-facing applications. It provides scalable identity solutions for millions of users, supports sign-up/sign-in with social accounts, email/password credentials, multifactor authentication (MFA), and highly customizable user journeys.

Key Differences:

Feature	Azure AD	Azure AD B2C
Target Audience	Internal users	External (customers, citizens)
Identity Providers	AAD, B2B	Local, Social, Enterprise
Custom Policies	Limited	Full via Identity Experience Framework
Branding Capabilities	Basic	Full HTML/CSS/JS customization
MFA	Strong, conditional access	Basic (SMS, Authenticator app)

What is a User Flow vs. a Custom Policy?

User Flows are built-in templates for common identity tasks such as sign-up, sign-in, password reset, and profile editing. They require no code and are configured using the Azure portal.

Custom Policies (also called Identity Experience Framework policies) offer complete control over every step of the identity journey. They're defined in XML and support advanced scenarios like REST API integration, external claims validation, and identity transformation.

When to Use Each:

- Use **User Flows** for standard use cases and fast setup.

- Use **Custom Policies** for advanced business rules, API calls, or multi-tenant configurations.

Can I migrate from User Flows to Custom Policies later?

Yes. Many organizations start with User Flows to get started quickly and migrate to Custom Policies once they need more control.

However, there's no automated migration tool. The migration requires:

1. Reviewing the current User Flow settings.

2. Replicating their logic using XML-based Custom Policies.

3. Testing the journey end-to-end.

4. Updating application configurations to point to the new policy.

Can I use Azure AD B2C in a multi-tenant SaaS app?

Yes, but with some limitations. Azure AD B2C is itself a **single-tenant directory**, but it can support multi-tenant **customers** by:

- Creating user journeys that detect tenant domains dynamically.

- Using custom policies with REST APIs to map tenant IDs to branding and policies.

- Allowing each tenant to sign in using their preferred identity provider (including federated Azure AD tenants via OpenID Connect or SAML).

How can I debug issues with Custom Policies?

Azure AD B2C provides detailed logging and error responses, especially when Application Insights is enabled.

Debugging Tips:

- Enable App Insights with your policy using the `<InstrumentationKey>` element.

- Inspect logs for orchestration step failures, REST call responses, and claim outputs.

- Use the **Run Now** button in the portal for real-time debugging.

- Return custom error messages using `<DisplayControl>` and `ErrorMessage` output claims.

Why is my token missing certain claims?

This typically happens due to one of the following:

- The claim is not mapped in the **OutputClaims** section of your technical profile.

- The claim was not included in the `scope` or `claims` parameter during token request.

- The application manifest does not list the claim as `optionalClaims`.

Ensure Output Mapping:

```
<OutputClaim ClaimTypeReferenceId="email" PartnerClaimType="email" />
```

Ensure Scope Includes Required Claims:

```
scope=openid profile email
```

Can I use Azure AD B2C with mobile apps?

Absolutely. B2C supports mobile platforms via MSAL libraries:

- **iOS:** MSAL for Objective-C/Swift

- **Android:** MSAL for Java/Kotlin

- **React Native:** MSAL browser-based or AuthSession with Expo

- **Flutter:** Via plugins like `appauth`

Use **Authorization Code with PKCE** for native apps to enhance security.

How can I support multiple languages in the sign-in experience?

Azure AD B2C supports localization through:

- **Built-in User Flows**: Enable languages via the Azure portal (Localization tab).

- **Custom Policies**: Use `<LocalizedResources>` in your `TrustFrameworkExtensions.xml`.

Sample:

```
<LocalizedResources Id="api.signup.en">

  <LocalizedStrings>

    <LocalizedString                          ElementType="UxElement"
StringId="email_entry">Enter your email address</LocalizedString>

  </LocalizedStrings>

</LocalizedResources>
```

You can even use a REST API to return dynamic localization values based on user country, preferences, or tenant.

What's the best way to manage environments (Dev/Test/Prod)?

Use separate Azure AD B2C tenants for each environment to maintain isolation.

- **CI/CD Pipelines**: Automate XML policy deployment using GitHub Actions or Azure DevOps.

- **Service Principals**: Use role-based access to manage each tenant securely.

- **Environment-Specific Config**: Store environment URLs and policy names in config files or Azure App Configuration.

Can I integrate custom APIs during sign-up or sign-in?

Yes. Use **RESTful API Connectors** in Custom Policies.

Common uses:

- Fraud detection
- Pre-filling claims
- Consent capture
- Email validation

Example TechnicalProfile:

```xml
<TechnicalProfile Id="REST-CheckUser">
  <DisplayName>Check User</DisplayName>
  <Protocol Name="Proprietary" />
  <Metadata>
    <Item Key="ServiceUrl">https://api.example.com/checkuser</Item>
    <Item Key="SendClaimsIn">Body</Item>
  </Metadata>
  <InputClaims>
    <InputClaim ClaimTypeReferenceId="email" />
  </InputClaims>
</TechnicalProfile>
```

How do I add a custom attribute like "Company Name"?

1. Add the attribute to your B2C tenant under **User Attributes**.

2. Reference it as a ClaimType in TrustFrameworkExtensions.xml.

3. Include it in the input/output of relevant policies.

4. Set   the   value   via   UI   or   API.

Example ClaimType:

```
<ClaimType Id="extension_companyName">

  <DisplayName>Company Name</DisplayName>

  <DataType>string</DataType>

</ClaimType>
```

What's the limit on users, policies, and REST calls?

Azure AD B2C is built for scalability, but there are limits:

- **Users**: Millions per tenant
- **Policies**: 100+ (can vary per region)
- **REST API Calls**: Limited to 5 calls per orchestration step
- **Token Lifetime**: Default is 60 minutes (configurable)

Always check the latest Azure AD B2C service limits.

Can I use biometric authentication with B2C?

B2C doesn't support native biometrics, but you can combine it with:

- **Device-level biometrics** via local authentication after token issuance (in mobile apps).
- **WebAuthn (FIDO2)**: Not natively supported in B2C, but it's on the roadmap.

Some developers simulate biometrics using app-level flows combined with short token lifetimes.

Why do I get an "AADB2C90077" error?

This common error means the requested policy does not exist or is not properly configured.

Checklist:

- Check spelling of the policy name in the URL
- Make sure the policy exists in the tenant
- Verify the application is registered for that policy

Is it possible to federate with another Azure AD tenant?

Yes. You can federate with external Azure AD tenants using **OpenID Connect** or **SAML** in a custom policy.

Federation allows external enterprise users to authenticate using their existing Azure AD credentials, while B2C still manages the UI and token issuance.

How can I test my policies locally?

While you can't run B2C policies entirely offline, you can:

- Use tools like **Postman** to simulate token flows
- Mock REST APIs with **httpbin** or **requestbin**
- Use **Application Insights** to simulate responses
- Apply changes in **Dev tenant** first and validate

Can I enforce Terms of Service acceptance?

Yes, using a combination of:

- A `ContentDefinition` to display HTML
- A Boolean claim (e.g., `extension_termsAccepted`)

- REST   API   or   session   claim   to   log   timestamp

This ensures users cannot continue without explicitly agreeing to terms.

Can I use Azure B2C in combination with Azure API Management (APIM)?

Yes. This is a common architecture.

- Use   B2C   to   authenticate   and   issue   tokens.

- Configure   APIM   to   validate   the   JWT   from   B2C.

- Use   scopes   and   roles   to   authorize   access   to   API   products.

These FAQs serve as both a rapid reference and a deeper dive into the most critical questions developers and architects face when working with Azure AD B2C. As the platform evolves, always refer to the official documentation and changelogs for updates and breaking changes.

www.ingramcontent.com/pod-product-compliance
Lightning Source LLC
LaVergne TN
LVHW051430050326
832903LV00030BD/3012